Austin James was born in a sleepy town in Wales. He overcame polio at age two with no more than a secondary education and without much prospect of employment in the area. He travelled across the newly built Severn Bridge opened in 1969 to an apprenticeship on Concorde, at Filton, before moving on to a twenty-two-year career with British Airways, London, another difficult move, then becoming Chief Flying Instructor for Cloud Base Aviation, a company he set up, over the past 36 years. He tells of the interesting stories and pitfalls that come with that life of adventure.

Austin James

LIVING THE DREAM!

AUSTIN MACAULEY PUBLISHERS®

LONDON * CAMBRIDGE * NEW YORK * SHARJAH

A CIP catalogue record for this title is available from the British Library.

ISBN 9781035879816 (Paperback)
ISBN 9781035879823 (Hardback)
ISBN 9781035879830 (ePub e-book)

www.austinmacauley.com

First Published 2024
Austin Macauley Publishers Ltd®
1 Canada Square
Canary Wharf
London
E14 5AA

Many thanks to Philip Baxter for his technical help and help with chapterising *Living the Dream!*.

Table of Contents

Foreword   9

Prologue   10

Chapter One: My Early Days: Schoolboy, Aircraft Engineer, Pilot   15

Chapter Two: My Apprenticeship   19

Chapter Three: The Engineer   27

Chapter Four: The New Job   36

Chapter Five: Another New Job   53

Chapter Six: A Second Change of Direction   61

Chapter Seven: My Start on the Road to Being a Pilot   68

Chapter Eight: My Pilot's Licence Arrives   75

Chapter Nine: Horizons: Becoming an Instructor   83

Chapter Ten: Our Club in the Southeast Corner   86

Chapter Eleven: Boy Gets Unplanned,
                         Very Long Air Experience Flight   106

Chapter Twelve: The Spanish Connection   108

Chapter Thirteen: Attention from 'The Powers That Be'   114

Chapter Fourteen: The Excitement Starts   119

Chapter Fifteen: The Excitement Continues   126

Chapter Sixteen: And So It Goes On!   137

Chapter Seventeen: Yet More Adventures!   141

Chapter Eighteen: Dangling Carburettor and Other Stories 149

**Chapter Nineteen: The Last Days of Shadow
                Manufacture and Various Repairs**   159

Chapter Twenty: The Dream Continues   163

Epilogue   174

Foreword

Microlight aircraft flying has bought flying within the reach of the ordinary man like myself in that you could cheaply learn to fly and buy your own aircraft if you so desired for the price of an average new car; the aircraft were slow at that time but that didn't matter as the joy of flight is similar to that thrill the Wright Brothers must have enjoyed all those years ago and is now available to anyone who wants to put the time in to learn and get his or her pilot's licence.

Prologue

Just Another Day at the Office

It was 18 July 2018, almost midday—and hot, around thirty-three degrees Celsius. I had just flown with my student, John, over the Surrey and Kent countryside, flying around Bough Beech Reservoir and looking at the hedge maze as we circled Hever Castle. Another successful pilot training lesson completed, teaching this student how to turn and climb the aircraft.

After we landed, I bade farewell to John, and before the next student arrived for the next flight, I thought about how, for the next flight, I could devise a detachable bigger scoop on my sliding window to make it scoop more air to make me—and the cockpit—generally cooler. However, before I could give that matter more thought, my next student, Paul, had arrived, so I gave up on that for the time being.

Paul was waiting for me with his son, in the cafe attached to our hangar. It was his first lesson, and he had never flown before with me, in our 'Flight Design CT', a three-axis microlight having just two seats side by side and an 'all-up' maximum weight of 450 kilograms (kgs).

I sat Paul in the left-hand seat (which is where the pilot-in-command sits when flying solo or with a passenger and where the student sits, the instructor occupying the right-hand seat). Just as in a car, pilots and passengers are obliged to secure themselves by seat belts—so I demonstrated the use of the CT's four-point harnesses, got him belted up, closed his door and belted myself into the right-hand seat.

I started the engine and carried on through the checklist before getting permission to taxi to holding point for the active runway. Runways are numbered according to the direction of the centreline (or imaginary centreline on a grass runway) with reference to Magnetic North, and the runway in use on this day was 'zero-eight right' (08R), which is the right-hand runway of the two east-west runways which were 08R and 08L (Magnetic North moves continuously relative to True North), and these runways are now designated 07(R) and 07(L).

At the hold and introducing Paul to the benefits of using a checklist, we completed our checks, increasing the engine revolutions ('revving' the engine) to 3500 RPM and trying each of the two separate ignition systems. We put the flaps to the take-off position, checked the flying controls for smooth and unrestricted operation, and we were then ready to line up on runway 08R.

Redhill Aerodrome is a big London airfield. It has an 'air traffic service' with air traffic controllers—not all airfields do—and they operate from a control tower. The 'tower' gave us permission to line up and then take off. As we rolled, the speed built up quickly, and we were soon into the climb.

All was going well—but *then*, I spotted smoke coming from the instrument panel, and the smell of burning was suddenly very strong! We were only about 600 ft into the climb, about 400 ft above the ground at Redhill, which is some 240 ft above mean sea level.

I thought for a second and then pressed the red (radio transmission) button on the control column: "Mayday! Mayday! Calling a Mayday!" is the most important call you can make, so important that it's the only time it is acceptable to break into a conversation while another pilot or The air traffic controller is talking. It also means that because you are in trouble, you own the airfield so to speak, and thus, you can do what you must to bring your aircraft down and save your life.

"Golf Papa, Papa, electrical fire!"

Immediately after that call, I could feel heat burning my left leg, well away from where the smoke was being emitted between the instrument 'mushroom' panel and the windscreen. I automatically lowered the nose and reduced engine power by 'throttling back', and turned the aircraft to the left, realising that a fire was on the other side of the thin sheet of carbon fibre that was right next to my left leg.

I put the aircraft in a steep left turn and spoke again to the tower controller, who had been silent after my emergency 'Mayday' call.

Thinking ahead during the turn, I thought that while both my student and I would, I hoped, escape the aircraft on landing, we would quite likely lose the aircraft—being able only to watch it burn, so thinking ahead, I told Paul, the air traffic controller as I turned back towards the runway, that I *did* need the aerodrome fire service. He quickly replied, "Yes, I know, they are coming!"

Paul the air traffic controller later told me that he had realised the seriousness of this emergency as he, too, could see the smoke billowing from my aircraft soon after we made the 'Mayday' call. I completed my turn, so I was now parallel and very close to the runway; it had been only about three minutes since we had taken off.

I decided to land halfway down the same runway which we had taken off as it fitted in with my emergency plan and would get us back on the ground in the shortest time!

One little problem we always have with the CT, which is normally beneficial, is that it is such a good glider, so it takes time to lose height even when the engine fails—not so valuable an asset when your leg is smouldering and you need to land quickly.

The smoke was now staining my windscreen, and my leg was burning. The landing circuit, as we call it, is normally of a rectangular shape, the first turn after take-off being 'crosswind', next turn being 'downwind'—parallel to the runway with wind on your tail—the third turn being the base leg with the final turn onto the runway centreline for the final approach to land. Well, that's how it works on normal occasions, but this was not normal, so my rectangle was more like a circle, if you get the drift; no time did we fly beyond the airfield boundary.

With the aircraft positioned 'late downwind and about to fly over the cafe', I selected the flaps to a landing position, forty degrees. I admit now that in the heat of the moment (little pun there), I nearly forgot to set landing flap altogether! As it was, it didn't really matter what flap setting I selected as, unbeknownst to me, the wiring had burnt out, so the flaps, although selected, remained as were, in the take-off position, giving me much more lift than I wanted for a landing.

By this time, I had flown a very short base leg and was about to turn onto 'final' (final approach to the runway in use) and lock on to the runway centreline—now, monitoring the aircraft's flying speed was crucial, especially so close to the ground. Not enough airspeed and the aircraft would stall, fall from the sky and explode; too much airspeed and the aircraft would crash-land or overshoot the runway, and in either case, most likely also end up in a ball of flame. Another thing on my mind was that the wings of the CT contained the fuel—a lot of it—that was piped down from the wings via a fuel filter to the fuel cock in the mushroom panel which, of course, was now on fire. There were about fifty litres of fuel just waiting to get us, and now, the smoke was getting so bad that I was struggling to read the most important instrument to the pilot—the airspeed indicator.

Anyway, we had to land, and land quickly. I had to 'feel' the aircraft onto the ground. The controls of the CT are very light and sensitive, but the aircraft will not do the landing for you. It is slippery. In other words, you have to work at the landing, because the aircraft likes to keep flying, especially if your approach speed is a little fast and worse if you think you have landing flap of forty degrees selected but in fact you are landing with take-off flap.

We were now on the runway centreline, about a third of the way along. It's easier to manoeuvre and aim to land midpoint down the runway, making a shallow turn in an emergency when it is long enough, and—thankfully—I knew that Runway 08R *was* long enough. Although I had not noticed them, we luckily did have the aerodrome fire service chasing close behind us, and after a few seconds more, the wheels were on the ground, just past the halfway point along runway 08R. I applied the brakes—really quite hard! After an adrenaline pause, I told my student to quickly get out of the aircraft.

We both vacated the aircraft very quickly and, once outside with both 'gullwing' doors open and a super-efficient fireman running up with a carbon dioxide (CO2) extinguisher in his hand, we sprayed the CO2 through a convenient hole in the mushroom panel—and hey, presto—the fire was out, fuel lines intact.

After we had disconnected the battery to avoid any possibility of the electrical fire reigniting, the fire service towed the aircraft with me inside, steering again back to the hangar.

I did confirm after looking at the flaps on the aircraft that the flaps, while selected to the chosen landing position (forty degrees), had in fact remained at take-off position, fifteen degrees.

 No time to rest on one's laurels: after 36 years of flying, having 14 engine failures and various emergencies, and after I had asked new student, Paul, if he was OK, I left GKUPP and sat him in our other aircraft, apologised to my next student—who was sitting outside the cafe drinking coffee—to say that we were now running a bit late! He told me that I had flown right over his head, billowing smoke! Not a good advert for the school for this day, methinks! (But I'm glad to say that he wasn't discouraged from flying by having seen that little escapade). I then strapped myself in next to Paul, and off we went again in our other CT.

After that little bit of excitement, the flying was good and uneventful, but of course, as I landed back at Redhill, the Air Accident Investigation Branch

(AAIB) was on to me, and I now had a load of paperwork to do, making a report about the incident.

One important thing I was unaware of but later told by the aircraft repairer was, that the fire, while burning my leg, had also almost burnt through the thin throttle cables, which also ran from the throttle on the centre console between pilot and passenger (instructor and student in this case) to the twin carburettors on the engine. Had they broken, or otherwise failed, the engine would have accelerated to full power as it is spring-loaded to do that for safety in normal times. If that had happened just as we touched down, we really would have been in the poo!

Welcome to the exciting world of aviation! "What was it that lead me here?" I hear you ask. I'll tell you.

Chapter One
My Early Days: Schoolboy, Aircraft Engineer, Pilot

I was born in 1953 in a little town in Wales; that was always undecided as to whether Chepstow was in Wales or in England. In 1955, at the age of two, I unfortunately contracted polio which, luckily, affected only my right leg and right foot. Nevertheless, I have walked with a limp from my right leg from that day to this. My parents told me that polio was so rare that our village doctors had no experience of the disease: in fact, my mother told me that initially, my doctor had told her to just give me junior aspirin.

She told me later that I cried with pain and had no strength in my right leg. It was only later, when my mother insisted on a second opinion from the other doctor in the practice, and after *that* doctor—also without experience of this disease—had visited and started to play ball with me, that I was rushed into the isolation ward in hospital. They thought my older sibling had bought the polio virus home from her school in Caldicot, and the school was then quarantined until the virus source was traced. There were about three of us in Chepstow who had contracted polio, luckily, and we were indeed fortunate that there were not more cases. I had to wear a leg-iron to support my right leg. But of the three of us, I escaped lightly—ending up with a thinner and three quarter of an inch shorter right leg than my left leg and my right foot arched, so not flat.

Polio is a serious muscle-wasting disease, but luckily, with advances in vaccination, exceedingly rare now. I had to wear that leg-iron for many years and be operated on, and oh! How I was glad when I was free of that dreaded iron.

When I was around thirteen, I had to go back into the hospital to have metal staples put into the bone in my good left leg. The operation had to be conducted at a crucial time, and I remember the surgeon telling my parents to rearrange our holiday, as time was critical to stop my good leg growing during the last period of height growth and let my right leg catch up.

I never realised that as a teenager, there is an age when your height is dictated and that's it, you are 5 ft 11.

Those days were quite different from how it is today, as I spent about ten weeks in traction at the hospital which, in itself for a young lad, was torture. Luckily, with new advances in medicine, one would never have to endure that now.

I doubt that many treatments could be regarded as enjoyable, but there was one that I recall as being in that category when I was very young before my teens. The lady physiotherapist in charge of my rehabilitation got me to put my cold leg into a heated wax bath at St Lawrence Hospital, Chepstow. *That* was lovely: my leg was coated with warm, thick wax that had to be peeled off later—but that was heaven!

After the latter operation to my good leg to insert the staples in my knee bone once healed, the nurses and doctors stood me on the table during my subsequent outpatient visits, and I had various height blocks of a quarter, half and three-quarter inches slipped under my right foot so that they could work out whether my hips lined up and whether my legs were even length—but nevertheless, to this day, I still sport a limp as I walk.

Now that I am getting old, my operations on my legs are coming back to haunt me in the form of arthritis in my knee and aches in my polio foot from time to time—even with the aid of the specially shaped insole in my shoe which I never use. Yet, I also remember my surgeon had the same surname as mine: his name was Dr James, who, with the science current in 1955, did a fantastic job at correcting my damage from this terrible disease.

An extra funny story to add here relating to my leg is, when I was in my early sixties, I had an appointment with podiatry at the hospital, where I was hoping to get a new insole specially made for my right foot. The funny side was that when the doctor saw my thin leg, there was a huge sigh! It was so loud there was no hiding it and no explanation was needed.

I said to the doctor, "Doctor if you can't help me, don't worry; just say so, but I have managed to walk with my right leg for the past fifty-five years."

He said, "But you have no muscle in your leg."

I could see the doctor desperately looking to offer some sort of solution, so in the end, he just packed out my old insole, telling me to return if that worked, and he would make a completely new insole.

Of course, I never went back.

Suppose the start of my relationship with aeroplanes began as a young boy with my adventures in the Air Training Corps where, on occasions, I managed to go flying at an RAF station. RAF, St Mawgan, in its 'Chipmunk' aircraft—a single-engine, two-seats-in-tandem aeroplane used for many years as a basic trainer by the Royal Air Force. Two Chipmunks sit hangered even to this day at our aerodrome fifty-seven years later, reminding me of when I was a young boy in the Air Training Corps.

Of course, when it was your turn to fly with the RAF pilot, you were always asked if you wanted to do aerobatics, and unfortunately, a no seemed to fall on the pilot's deaf ear.

When I left school and it was decision time as to finding a career, it was evident that it was going to be something in engineering as I, as a child, had always liked to take things to pieces to find out how they worked: and I remember that my Meccano set was one of my favourite toys—it was an all-metal-parts, relatively complex construction kit of cogs, wheels, metallic strips of various shapes and sizes, and nuts and bolts, that it comprised.

You could build many mechanised cars, boats and cranes of anything you wanted, really, with an electric motor to make everything come to life.

When I was sixteen, of course, like every young lad, I wanted my own wheels to get around, but my requests for a motorbike were ignored, with my mum and dad telling me that they thought (and I agree now) that motorbikes are dangerous. My father instead bought me, from a mate in the pub, a cheap 1953 ex-General Post Office (GPO) 'Morris 1000' van with a BMC 803 cc engine with a 'split' (two-segment) windscreen—a banger to shut me up! It had rubber front wings strictly not legal now. I stripped the engine down and put it all back together.

I remember painting it 'post office' red outside and light grey inside and loved driving it up and down the 15-metre drive to our house, as at age sixteen, I had no driving licence, of course, but our short drive at our semi-detached was off-road, private land.

One day, I managed to completely turn my Morris through 180 degrees, with a hedge next to it on one side and the flower beds on the other side. There was about eighteen inches clear on each side: talk about a three-point turn; this must have been a fifty-point turn! My father, when he returned from work, was initially surprised though annoyed as he thought I had taken the van out on the road, then duly impressed—or was it unimpressed when I told him actually how I turned it—especially as the hedge was still standing and undamaged and the flower bed was untouched, too!

During World War II, my father was in the Merchant Navy. After the war, he worked for the 'red and white' bus company. He was not a mechanical man, but he reached 'Scheduling Manager' status with the company, having worked with the company for most of his life. He often told me of days when he had to go out in the snow, digging stranded buses out of the snow with nothing but 'elbow grease' and shovels.

I was now almost seventeen years old and about to leave school. Dad, knowing I loved mechanical things, wanted me to get a skill a trade as he thought that with a trade, you would always be in work.

My father's brother, my Uncle Pat, was a film editor with the British Broadcasting Corporation the BBC. Uncle Pat told my father as an alternative that he would try to get me into television as a cameraman but my father would have none of it; instead, he told me he would try to get me into the bus company as an apprentice diesel fitter at our local bus depot, but only, he said, as a last resort. When I asked why as a last resort, he told me that it was because the small bus company was about to be taken over by 'National Bus'; he didn't know the future; and that he wanted better things for me.

So, what to do, then? Well, I knew I wanted to use my hands and get an engineering job, and I liked aircraft and, luckily for me, fate played a hand. The Queen (that is, Her Late Majesty, Queen Elizabeth II) had just opened the Severn Bridge from the Chepstow side where I lived, to Filton, Bristol—where 'Rolls Royce Aero Engines' was; and on the same industrial site, next to Rolls Royce Aero Engines, was the British Aircraft Corporation (BAC), who were building the Concorde Supersonic Aeroplane. I remember, in the hot summer of my last days in school, British Aircraft Corporation's Test Pilot Brian Trubshaw flew the prototype Concorde over my back garden in Chepstow on its first test flight!

Chapter Two
My Apprenticeship

In early summer, I had applied for a career with both companies. I had interviews with both companies, but I also had to complete mechanical tests with British Aircraft Corporation as well. Unlike Rolls Royce Aero Engines, BAC company tests overruled your school achievements, so lucky for me, a good secondary education was good enough if you passed the tests.

It's funny how things work out. As luck would have it, I was accepted for an apprenticeship with both companies. As I was mad on engines, I had hoped to go to Rolls Royce—my first choice—but its offer was conditional upon my getting a high grade in English at school. Luckily, I had not put all my eggs in one basket, as unfortunately, I did not achieve that grade, so no job with Rolls Royce was offered. So, fate decided for me, and I was off to be an apprentice with BAC on the Concorde. Looking back, that turned out to be the much better option of the two as, in my apprenticeship years, after visiting Rolls Royce, I soon realised that working on a vast project aircraft like the Concorde was far the better choice than a jet engine that was the size of a small car.

One of the conditions told to me and my family was the British Aircraft Corporation insisted that I left home to take up my apprenticeship, so for the first time in my life, I was leaving my home, on my own in the wide world.

Unbeknownst to me, though, was the pact that my parents had made, to divorce when their last child had left home—and that was me my sister already having gone, now married. Of course, stupid young lad me, I only realised the coincidence of the break-up timing and the house for sale sign in later years.

BAC required me to live on site, at Bristol Filton Airport. There was a hostel, a big place, run by the YMCA but exclusively for apprentices from Rolls Royce and the British Aircraft Corporation for the first year. This was a new chapter in my life, to be sharing a room with two others: one from Liverpool and one lad from Swindon, who unfortunately had diabetes, having to inject himself with insulin. Going from school kid living at home to apprentice aircraft fitter was quite a jump; you had to grow up very fast! One thing in particular still reminds me of my days as an apprentice when I hear it now, and it is the song 'In The Summertime' by Mungo Jerry, playing on one of the walking apprentice's ghetto blasters at the start of my first year 1969 as we walked across Bristol Filton Airport, dodging the aircraft to get to work each morning.

I remember, too, that the warden at the hostel had a good-looking daughter. Unfortunately for me, though, there were about 120 young apprentices living there, so she was spoilt for choice, so to speak, as we all liked looking at her.

The BAC apprentices and the Rolls Royce lads were put into the Rolls Royce Technical College machine shop, a huge place with every type of machine for turning, grinding, drilling and shaping—in fact, every machine you might think of was in there. I remember that, for safety reasons (and a very clever idea it was too), there was a big red emergency 'STOP' button on every metal post. Pressing that button would immediately shut down every machine in the shop, and you can guess that, with a band of foolish young seventeen-year-olds, the machine shop came to an abrupt stop many times throughout the working day.

We had already been warned about the dangers of sticking a high-pressure air line up another apprentice's bum that it was dangerous, and as it had already been done with a poor lad ending up in hospital with a twisted bowel, stunts like that would have instantly ended your career, and it did for the perpetrator.

We had a few characters in our year of apprentices. One (let's call him Max) was more trouble than he was worth: if he was in your group, most of the time, he was up to no good. In the car park, on one occasion, he dismantled the 'Lambretta' scooter of a fellow apprentice. In the store, we could get a lump of plasticine and a pin (we called it a sticky pin); the idea was that on a pillar drill, when you put a large drill in the drill chuck, with the machine off, you could put the plasticine on the end of the drill, insert the pin in the plasticine, and with the machine on running slowly and a steel rule, you could get the pin to get the centre of the drill.

This would allow you to position your work piece to be drilled directly under your pin, and hence, the hole would be in exactly the correct position accurate to thousands of an inch—well, that was what the pin was intended to be used for, but Max's favourite trick was to put a pin and the plasticine on the emergency stop button on some poor apprentices milling machine so that when things went wrong, which happened often, and that poor person hit the stop button frantically, he would get a nasty stab and end up with a pin in his hand.

Pure evil or, at best, really stupid. We were very glad when we saw the back of him, but to our amazement, in later years, they made him an inspector.

Then, there was Tom, a very tall, nice lad. He became my good friend while I worked for BAC and beyond. Tom *did* get the English grade at school that had eluded me, and Tom worked for Rolls Royce Aero Engines, but we were together as apprentices for the first two years. I often felt sorry for Tom as the lads had nicknamed him 'Tommy Tear-Ass', the reason being that Rolls Royce Technical College workshop, as I have said, was huge with many big machines shaping, milling, grinding, drilling and turning. As part of our training, we moved around each section, being on that section for a week or perhaps two weeks, learning to, for example, master accurate internal or external grinding to tolerances of thousands of an inch.

At the end of the week, in line with City and Guilds' training standards, we were given what they called a Phase Test. This involved being given a drawing and having to make apart from that drawing, to high specification. This, of course, normally involved multiple operations unique to equipment on that section, and a specific time was allocated for this work. It was, after all, a test.

Poor old Tom, and unfortunately did it so many times that he would race ahead well in advance of all of us: when I had just completed the third stage of the job, Tom would be finishing the fourth stage; everyone would be jealously remarking how fast Tom was. This happened so many times, but as Tom got to the last stage of the Phase Test, we couldn't help ourselves but to laugh, for we would all be alerted by a horrendous graunching sound as Tom's work piece was annihilated by his machine, normally because he was attempting to rush and take too much metal off the piece in one go.

The cutter would jam and anialate the work, and that was it. As the graunching died down, Tom's work was seen to be scrap, and I remember every Section Instructor, no matter how mild-mannered, shouting at him. For poor old Tom, it was a regular event mark for Phase Test zero: Tim from hero to zero in one instant.

The apprenticeship years went on, and because I was born in Chepstow, there was always a question as to whether I was Welsh or English. Chepstow was on the border, but though my father and grandparents were Welsh, my mother was a Londoner. I had a Welsh accent, and because of that, I got called 'Taffman' which, of course, I hated, but couldn't do much about. There was one particular apprentice, though, Neville, who could not stop baiting me: whether he thought it improved his standing in the pack having a go at me, I don't know. How does a bully's mind work?

I realised though, in hindsight, that he did me a favour, as I was now in a similar situation to that which I had experienced at secondary school: I was bullied so much then that it affected me, making me nervous and stressed. That particular school bully even used to wait for me to get off the school bus each morning before taunting me and punching me.

Looking back, I took this bullying for far too long before I finally blew up and thumped him! It's funny in that then when retaliating, I realised how weak these people are, that these people are cowards with problems that make them as they are. I was not ever bullied at school after that—but now, here it was again; the same sort of intimidation was happening to me with Neville.

During one particular week, we were in the aircraft fitting section of the technical college where they had built the building around a big aeroplane, a piston-engine 'Percival Provost' that had a retractable undercarriage and where we were mainly learning about hydraulics. In this department, there was also a special rig set up with a main undercarriage from a 'Bristol Britannia', an old commercial airliner, that could be retracted or extended at the touch of a lever on the wall—very impressive, and it taught us a lot about hydraulic systems.

For example, we soon realised that a minute particle of dirt in a pipe coupling would inevitably leak profusely with 3000 pounds per square inch of hydraulic pressure put on it.

Anyway, I digress.

There was a coffee bar in the college where we would all queue up for tea or coffee and hard cheese or ham rolls. Almost every day, I would be sitting in the café, eating and drinking, and a crust of roll would fly across the cafe and hit me in the head or body. This went on for some time, and foolishly, I put up with these taunts—that was, until one particular day.

The cafe was full, no empty seats, so I was sitting on the floor, my back against the corridor wall. The corridor was stacked out with apprentices, and while I was enjoying my coffee, this bloody crust flew at me and hit me in the face. Well, at this point, my fuse blew, the adrenalin level ran high, and I got up, lunged at Neville, and fists were flying. He was overwhelmed, I was in a frenzy, and he was the loser. He wasn't the hero he thought he was, and I was so mad I can't remember feeling any of his punches if he managed to land any on me.

I distinctly remember, though, there was now this big mass of apprentices around us, shouting, "Fight, fight!" as, of course, weird seventeen-year-olds always do: after all, this was free entertainment. Neville ended up a crumbling mass on the floor and later sported a black eye. Then, I remember the bell going off to get us to return to work, though too late to save this bully.

Once I had cooled down, I was really worried. I thought how stupid I had been in that I had lost control, and I could be in big trouble. Thinking the worst, I could lose my job, a job I loved and had worked so hard to get; and I worried that that being the case, how disappointed my dad would be; he had invested in me, even bringing me to the interview.

I returned to the aircraft fitting shop and awaited my fate, but my fate never came. I was not summoned, nothing was said; it was as if it had never happened; gosh I was so lucky! I can only speculate that this was because it was so out of character for me to lose my temper and or do something bad like that, but with all the noise, it could not have gone unnoticed. I can only surmise that the college staff decided best to leave the incident be.

Well, Neville never threw anything at me again and even problematic Max, after being one of the unruly spectators of the fight, decided never to try any of his antics or horseplay on me. From that day on, my attitude changed with regards to turning the other cheek too many times.

After the Provost shop, I remember enjoying my time in the welding department of the college where we learnt how to do oxyacetylene welding and brazing. The reason I mention it is that we couldn't avoid a lot of blowbacks, and burning ourselves regularly was par for the course.

After two years at the technical college, we were released to be assigned with the fitters in the factory. Of course, as the fitters were on bonus, they didn't always want a spotty apprentice working with them, but like it or not for them, we were, at last, let loose on Concorde Production doing two weeks in the factory and one week back at the technical college.

How lucky I was in working at British Aircraft Corporation, which was confirmed later when the Rolls Royce apprentices and I went from the technical college to visit each factory, and I realised that Tom was working on an engine the size of a small car while I was working in a vast assembly hall called the

Brabazon Hangar on a huge Concorde Aircraft 002—and to me, that was much more exciting. Funny how circumstances out of your control map your life.

The plan set for us now was to complete our Engineering Training Board modules, which meant that we had to learn many skills, from drilling precisely to bending metal into components, to size, to flange and dimple metal and rivet fuselage skins, all that in the fitting shop where we built aircraft components. In fact, I can say we had a go at everything.

There was, though, one place where none of us wanted to go. That place was the Press Shop. That shop, we deemed, was the most boring workplace because, whenever we had visited it, all we saw was a dingy-looking shop with a bunch of old men, some asleep—no offence intended; after all, I am old now myself—bending metal: and it looked boring, so we tended to book our two weeks' annual leave when we were on the plan to go there as part of our training.

We didn't get out of it, though; you had to do your two weeks in the Press Shop. Like it or not, they would get you in there eventually.

There was also a period when the apprentice training school struggled to find places in the factory for all the apprentices, though these were situations that didn't happen often. On one occasion, I was asked to join plant maintenance for a while, which was a good number—plenty of tea breaks, repairing anything that broke down in the factory.

One day, the fitter I was with had to change the flag on the flagpole. He said to me, "Up you go, lad," as I climbed the steel ladder concreted into the top of the building. Well, I wasn't good at heights, funny becoming chief flying instructor in later life, and it became inevitable that with me frozen to the ladder, it was not a good look and wouldn't get the flag sorted, so my mentor would shout to get me down and take over. I am afraid to say, on that day, I fell apart like a cheap watch.

On another occasion, they asked me if I would go into the company garage and work on the company cars and vans and forklifts and in fact everything else with wheels. I loved that, as I had a little Frog Eye Sprite sports car and it meant that I could, unlike the other apprentices, park my car behind the garage inside the factory. It was surreal that a 1950s-looking garage was lost inside this vast aircraft factory.

My mentor in the garage was a man called John Kaman who was, I think, the best mechanic in the garage. He taught me a lot, but I was already very good on cars because, at 16, as you may recall, my father had bought me that old ex-

General Post Office Morris van with an 803-cc engine, a split windscreen and the rubber wings—so I had a bit of hands-on experience.

In the BAC garage, we did all our own stuff, everything from skimming cylinder heads, grinding-in valves and changing tyres. It was embarrassing, though, when soon after starting in the garage, I was given the simple task of putting antifreeze into all the company directors' chauffeur-driven cars, only to have these cars all return to the garage under tow after having broken down through overheating *and* while the company directors were in them! How embarrassing! What I didn't know then, which I was never told, and I know now, is that you need to run the engine with the radiator cap off to let all the air out after you add antifreeze to the radiator. Oops!

Part of the garage included the motor electricians' section for rewiring generators and refurbishing them. In this section, there was an electrician called Raymond who sadly had Parkinson's disease which, over time, was getting worse, and sometimes, we would hear a loud shout just before a generator flew across the garage in a throw, which was beyond Raymond's control from his inadvertent, uncontrolled, spasms, bless him.

I liked Ray. He was a nice, funny guy who showed me the inner workings of a generator. (We didn't have alternators then). Unfortunately, as Ray's Parkinson's got worse, the company had to retire him for health and safety reasons.

The managing director of BAC had a metallic gold, chauffeur-driven 'E-Type' Jaguar, which was brand-new, and it came into the garage, where John Kaman was only allowed to do minor tasks, because it was deemed that the main dealers should do the regular maintenance and servicing. Evidently, the thinking was that the various jobs to be done were too specialised for John. That stood until the director caught one of the apprentices at the Main Dealer working on his car, so that was the end of that and, from then on, John took charge of all the E-Type maintenance and repairs.

Got on well in the garage. I enjoyed it and worked hard. The manager of the garage liked my work, and one day, he called me into the office, where he asked me if I would like to change my apprenticeship from an aircraft one to that of a motor mechanic—and stay in the garage for good. I was an eighteen-year-old, and the offer was very tempting, for I loved it in there, but after being in turmoil and speaking to my dad about the offer, he was realistic, and we decided that changing my apprenticeship from being an aircraft engineer to that of a motor fitter was perhaps not a wise move in the long term and that, I *think*, turned out to be the right decision.

Anyway, I completed my aircraft apprenticeship and became a skilled aircraft fitter working on this prestige aircraft, Concorde, the world's first supersonic airliner—whoopee!

Eventually, I got to stay in the assembly hall and work on the aircraft in its entirety, helping to build it.

Chapter Three
The Engineer

Most of the guys smoked in those days—luckily for me, after trying to be cool like my mates and trying a packet of Peter Stuyvesant cigarettes and then forgetting I had them in the car glove compartment, I didn't bother—but friends Ben and John smoked like chimneys, and for the smokers, the company provided a metal-fenced area in the corner of the hangar, which we aptly named the pig pen.

In those days, the 1970s, the factory operated a bonus scheme, and all the fitters worked on what was called 700 percent bonus. That was the maximum they could achieve to earn maximum salary. It was strange but worked like this: when a drawing for a production job came out for the first time, the 'rate-fixer' (the person who estimated a time and cost for the job) had no idea how long the job would take to do, so he would be obliged to estimate a number of hours or days to allocate to this job. The task would then be given to the aircraft fitter. He would try to do the job as quickly as he could, hoping to make good money, seven hundred percent, if possible, on the bonus for that job.

Of course, if the fitter did the job in a seventh of the time—that is, with a seven hundred percent bonus—the rate-fixer would try to save money the next time that that job came out, and he would secretly reduce the job time substantially. The next aircraft fitter asked to do that job would have no chance of doing it in anything like the allotted time and so, would make no bonus at all! When this happened, the fitter would be forced to go to the rate-fixer and beg for more time. This made it appear that he was slow, even when he was not.

Of course, if the fitter found out that the job had had seven times the amount of time allocated for it when it first emerged, he would be really angry with the rate-fixer and tempers got heated; so, the bonus scheme was never a good idea, and it caused a lot of arguments between fitter and rate-fixer. Sometimes, they almost came to blows.

The bonus scheme, created to be an incentive to work harder, worked against safety. One example of safety being seriously compromised occurred with the Concorde. The aircraft's major fuselage and wing sections came from France (or from Weybridge) to be joined. They were flown-in on 'Guppy' transport aircraft, a peculiar, wide-bodied transport aircraft used for carrying extra-large items of cargo. In big sections, the front of the Guppy including the Pilots Cockpit hinged open with the cockpit facing the tail. These sections were then mounted on 'jigs in the assembly hall'—painted orange—which were concreted into the hangar floor. These large sections of wing included fuel tanks. These and the sections of the fuselage were joined by chemically etched wing planks.

BAC had developed a method where a wing panel would be coated with designated areas of like a rubber coating and then the panel would be immersed in an acid. The acid removed about one thousandths of an inch of thickness off the panel per hour except for the parts that were protected by the special coating, hence the name chemical etching, this allowed the aluminium alloy panels to be made with intricate detail and strength. Then, when the aircraft fuselage and wing sections came together on the orange jigs, the edges of the planks joined the aircraft sections by overlap joints—about two inches of plank overlapping each section. As the whole wing was a fuel tank, there was a need to seal it on assembly and a rubbery substance (called sealant!) was used in the joint.

Now, to get thicknesses precise, the company had a machine that made this rubbery sealant and sandwiched it between two pieces of nylon tape. This sealant had the consistency of chewing gum, sandwiched between two rolls of nylon tape; and the advantage of this was that the machine produced a uniform, precise, thickness of sealant about ten thousandths of an inch as it left the machine—perfect for a professional uniform fuel tight joint.

The idea was that the fitters would first *meticulously* clean the mating surfaces with a solvent, peel off one side of the tape, stick the bare sealant onto the lap edge, cut to length and then, lastly, peel off the top side of tape, leaving a nice layer of black sealant on the surface of the lap joint before putting the wing plank down, joining the sections together and then fitting the bolts and rivets. Simples, yes? Well, no!

Done properly, this produces a uniform ten-thousandth of an inch sandwich of sealant to seal the joint. Now, here lies the problem, because if the fitters were on bonus, they had a tendency to cut corners to finish the job quickly, and they would rush the solvent cleaning and, as they put the tape down in some uncleaned places, of course, on a greasy surface, it wouldn't stick. The sealant would break as they peeled off the top layer of plastic, so the guys would then have to cut another piece of sealant tape and overlap the gaps with another length of tape, effectively making a bridge, and the overlapped ten-thousandths of an inch thick sealant became twenty-thousandths of an inch with a void underneath—or more, at the ends. All the taper-lock bolts and rivets would go in, and much later in the production process, when we got to test the tank for leaks, it would leak like a sieve!

Eventually, British Aircraft Corporation realised that the bonus scheme was costing them dearly, and a standard daily rate was introduced to replace it. This proved to be a much better idea, and there were then no more arguments with the rate-fixer, either.

I spent a lot of time working on the wings of Concorde, and fuel systems were my speciality. It was well-known that they housed all the fuel, and there were thirteen fuel tanks, ten in the wings and three in the fuselage. That said there were no separate fuel tanks, the structure itself was the fuel tank, and so, after building it, the structure had to be sprayed internally with rubber sealant and to make the structure fuel tight. Once this had been completed and the structure was ready for testing, we started the leak testing process by blanking off all the access panels with special blanks, then pumping the structure full of air so that, with the tank inflated, we could, with notebook and pen and a brush with a pot of soapy water, test and inspect every seam, every bolt, every rivet, looking for bubbles to indicate leaks. Of course, on that first look, we found hundreds of leaks, and each one had to be fixed.

It was very clever. We had a very high-powered Semco sealant gun that we connected to an airline and, in turn, to a 'banjo' bolt, one that had a small hole throughout its length and in its side. The idea was that we would remove an aircraft bolt or rivet that we suspected to be across the leak path, replace it temporarily with our little banjo bolt and its fibre washers, inject the sealant at about three thousand pounds per square inch pressure—a pressure so powerful as to squirt sealant between the skins—and that this would fill the void that was the leak.

On one strange occasion, I injected two guns full of sealant while looking inside the tank to search for a pool of black surplus gunge coming out of the void, and confirming I had fixed the leak, I found nothing! I then refilled and fired the gun again—nothing! I was bemused! It was only by chance that I stuck my head into a fuel tank some distance and not related to the leak where, to my amazement, there was a huge pool of sealant! The source of the leak was not only a long way from the leak apparent on the outside, but in a different tank! I couldn't believe it! That leak wasted loads of sealant, and I had a lot of cleaning up to do, and however hard you tried to keep the horrible black sealant off your hand, it was impossible, and it would not wash off for days.

Anyway, when we had reduced our long list of leaks to zero, having crossed off each one in our notebook, we went to phase two. We then pumped up the tank with air again. This time, mixing it with a little bit of freon gas, and this time we had a super-duper hot element 'sniffer' gun, which beeped when it sniffed the gas, we stumbled on a number of smaller leaks. You can now perhaps appreciate how our job became easier as there were fewer leaks once the bonus scheme was finally scrapped!

Concorde's fuel tanks inside contained a latticework of rods to provide strength to the wing. Each rod was of about two inches diameter and 'wasted' (i.e., tapered) towards the ends. They were fixed from the top, chemically etched skin web to the bottom skin web. I was skinny in those days (how I wish were now) so could slide through the elliptical tank-access panel and crawl between the pyramid-shaped gap of the lattice to the part of the tank that I needed to get into to work on or install a pump etc. When I got tired, which sometimes happened in the afternoon, I could position myself inside the tank, across the elliptical opening, and have a little sleep—knowing that because my body was horizontal, covering the access hole, somebody who was looking for me would have to poke me to get my attention.

Not for one minute did anyone suspect that one was in the land of Nod: the only thing I didn't consider, until many years later, was that had I snored, my snoring would have given the game away! That said, apart from the occasional afternoon nap, I did work hard and learnt a lot and enjoyed every minute of my time at BAC.

Building the Concorde involved much drilling, and when working in the fuselage, as fast as we drilled, there were three ladies with vacuum cleaners whose prime task was to constantly hoover up our 'swarf', swarf being the metal debris left after you drilled a hole. The women were stars in that they were impervious to all the bad language that came from many aircraft fitters when the job was not going quite the way it should have. Other engineers and motor mechanics will agree with this. There was a requirement for another cleaner and, sure enough, a new young girl started working on the aircraft armed with her new, trusty vacuum cleaner. The problem for this young woman working with hundreds of men was that she was far too pretty, and every time she walked across the hangar floor, everyone working on the Concorde stopped what they were doing and gaped at her. Sadly, for all of us, because of this, she didn't last the week! We enquired after her, of course, and management told everyone that she had unfortunately failed her medical—evidently, a most diplomatic answer.

My friend Ben, one of us four musketeers, was put to work on Concorde engine air intakes. He was not so happy about that. There were two pairs of intakes fitted to each Concorde. The twin intakes were about the size of a small fighter aircraft and were quite compact and complicated. The design again was quite clever with hydraulically controlled ramp doors and sensors; and lots of other rods and levers that made up these complicated parts. Fabricating and installing the intakes was a big job, rather like building a small jet aircraft, and the Concorde couldn't operate without them.

This is why. The Concorde was fitted with four Rolls Royce 'Olympus 593' jet engines two on each wing. A jet engine takes air in through the front and compresses it. The air then travels through restrictions called 'Venturies' (named after Giovani Venturi, the 18th century scientist who discovered some of the principal characteristics of fluid dynamics) and divergent ducts which speed up or slow down the air drawn in, increasing or decreasing its velocity, pressure and temperature. A rotating axial compressor compresses the air going into the engine, and as it goes through to the combustion section, fuel is added.

The fuel-air mixture thus created is then ignited, creating a vast superheated, pressurised expansion of gases, that are forced through a turbine, turning both it and the compressor which are joined together by a big shaft. Then, the jet-stream exhausts through an exhaust nozzle (the jet pipe) at great velocity, pushing the engine forward and, because the engine is fixed to the aircraft, off goes the aircraft with it. This force was discovered by Sir Isaac Newton and is stated as a 'law' in his Third Law Of Motion.

Newton's Third Law states that for every action, there is an equal and opposite reaction. An 'everyday' example of this is the motion of a balloon allowed to deflate suddenly: when you blow up a balloon and let it fly out of your hand without tying the nozzle, the air under pressure inside the balloon exhausts through the nozzle, and as the air gushes out, the balloon shoots off at a great speed. Movement of the gas backwards, relative to the balloon, creates equal movement of the balloon forwards, so that it flies uncontrolled until the air inside is exhausted. When I try this at a Christmas party, the balloon is normally constrained by the ceiling where, after making a funny farting noise, it deflates suddenly and falls to the floor. Well, an engine jet pipe acts like the balloon nozzle, and the exhaust gas exiting it is like the air leaving the balloon.

Well, back to Ben and the reason for positioning these heavy intakes in front of the jet engines. You may not be aware of this (few people are, and why should they be?) but a jet engine can only accept air flowing into it as long as its speed is no greater than half the speed of sound—that's me getting technical again. The speed of sound is approximately seven hundred and forty-nine miles per hour at sea level. That's when you hear the sonic boom, so for the engines, if the air is faster than about three hundred and seventy-five miles per hour, the jet engine cannot accept it. The engine would stall, and stop running i.e., 'flame out'. So, the question to be answered was, how could air going into the engines be slowed to less than half the speed of sound when the Concorde is travelling at four times that speed in supersonic flight (at twice the speed of sound)?

The 'boffins' devised an answer: you get the air intakes to slow down the air just before it enters the engine! Even cleverer than even I imagined, the intakes had computer-controlled ramp doors which, when in the correct position, produced an invisible shock wave that stood between the ramps. This shockwave acted like a giant filter, with supersonic air going through it at its front and air at half the speed of sound coming out of the shock wave at its back before going into the front of the engines.

Oh! And just one more thing about the engines: if you squirt more neat fuel into the hot jet stream, it ignites rapidly in the hot jet pipe. To do this, you add fuel injectors (known as a 'reheat' system) which then accelerates the Concorde from subsonic flight to supersonic flight—in a jiffy!

They call this afterburner, and one other thing—apart from the jet engines, a percentage of thrust was generated solely from the combination of the intake and the primary nozzle i.e. the jet pipe, brilliant technology.

Anyway, enough of the technical stuff. The *funny* bit I wanted to tell you, at long last, you say, was that when the intakes pairs were finally built and finished—and believe me, they took a long time—the company made a fascinating machine that lifted and rotated these intakes up and down, around and around, vertically and horizontally—in fact, through every angle you could imagine. Underneath the intake, they put a big, brown sheet of paper, and once the machine was switched on, there would be rivets and nuts and other pieces that fell out through the access panels. The machine ensured that no foreign objects were left in the internal parts of any set of intakes.

The finishing of a set of intakes drew a crowd to watch this marvellous machine in operation, and we could see the intake-builders, including my mate Ben, scared to death that one of his spanners that he might have mislaid weeks before would end up staring at him from the brown paper along with the rivets and other ejected debris. I expect you can guess that nobody etched their names on their spanners!

At that time, I had four really good friends, all apprentice aircraft fitters—except one, Ian, who, for some reason (and I believe it was poor attendance) had not completed his module training, so British Aircraft Corporation eventually downgraded his apprenticeship from skilled aircraft engineer to semiskilled tradesman. Ian then got a place at RAF Fairford, still working for British Aircraft Corporation—and a good place to be it was, as his father worked there too; and RAF Fairford was where the completed Concorde prototype was flight tested and flew from on its hot and high tours around the globe, looking for buyers with the Transport Minister on board, so most of the Fairford British Aircraft Corporation staff went along with the aircraft to maintain it on its travels, lucky devils.

So now, there were three 'musketeers'—Ben, John and me: we were not four anymore, and the three of us were left alone at Filton. We three remembered some good times on holiday in Jersey with Ian—he was a good-looking lad in his cream suit. One afternoon, though, while we worked on the Concorde, we got some really bad news.

At lunchtime, Ian had gone to the pub for lunch with a friend in Fairford village, and for some reason, Ian and his workmate had then decided to go out on the river in a small boat. Whether or not he had had a little bit too much to drink we never knew, but sadly, Ian fell overboard, and though, he was a good swimmer, they found his body at the bottom of the weir. Ian was twenty-one years old when we went to his funeral: his fiancée was there, too. This was indeed a very sad day.

My friends and I were very close, like brothers; and after five years on the Concorde, there were rumours that production of it was due to stop and that the future of the aircraft didn't look good, so us young, hot-headed lads decided to jump ship and do something else. We joined Westland Helicopters at Weston Super-mare. Unfortunately, being young, we stayed only a short time—in fact, only a matter of months, because we struggled with yet another bonus scheme. Truth was, we completed our jobs very quickly, but the system would not allow the company to pay us the bonus that we were due because we were on a probationary period designed to pay us a guaranteed amount while we got up to speed, problem was we were up to speed already.

Added to that, my friend Ben was promised that his position in the other hangar away from us, his mates, was only temporary. His manager liked his work and insisted on keeping him. Well, we were young and we were not having that, so we left Westland Helicopters, en masse. That caused a bit of a rumpus at the time. The Personnel Department was a little annoyed, to say the least, losing three skilled engineers at one hit—even asking us if we had mortgages! Well, at 21, what the hell were those? Leaving Westland's didn't go down well with Westlands.

We then enjoyed another holiday in Jersey as you do, our favourite destination. We had plenty of Jersey holidays then; oh, to be young and free, but reality hit me on return from Jersey. We had no job, and therefore, no income. I had a friend who told me his father worked for British Rail at its Bristol Bath Road Depot: it was really good money because of the shift work, and the railway needed people who had worked on air conditioning systems as the High-Speed Train was about to be introduced.

Three young aircraft engineers wanting jobs seemed to be a good picking, so there we were, blagging our way in, now not aircraft engineers but Diesel Traction Engineers, and that is where I stayed for two years. I hankered, though, to return to the aircraft industry, but my two friends were happy to keep their new high paid roles with British Rail.

There was one close shave when the manager threatened Ben with the sack when he seemed to be the only person alive who could walk through the filthy engine room of a Class Fifty locomotive, emerging from the other end with not a speck of oil or soot on his clothes or face and with every strand of his hair perfectly in place—in fact, looking as though he was just about to go clubbing! But after that reprimand, with him being watched closely, we made sure we touched him with our dirty hands every time we passed him to stop that problem ever happening again!

After a while, I was having withdrawal symptoms from not working on an aircraft. After all, in my mind, British Rail was meant to be a stop-gap job, so this was the end of the three musketeers as Ben and John remained happily working on the railway, while I got a job albeit with less money—a long way from Bristol—with British Airways London, at Heathrow Airport.

Chapter Four
The New Job

Times were hard from then on as I had not only to move from Bristol to London but also to find somewhere to live while I paid a mortgage on an empty house in Bristol. Luckily, or maybe not luckily, British Airways had a welfare office, and a nice lady in that office found me a small room at a house near the airport in Hayes, Middlesex. The only thing was that the landlady would not give any of her lodgers a key. Mrs Penhurst preferred renting to aircrew who only stayed for one or two nights before flying off for two weeks and then only stopped on return for one night before going home to Lancashire, or wherever. Of course, she favoured them as they paid for the days, and they didn't live there.

For her, I, being a greasy engineer, working days Monday to Friday in British Airways' workshops with no shift-pay 'coming home' each day, was not what she really wanted.

My housemate was a cabin steward. He enjoyed the large bedroom that he rarely occupied as he was always away flying. I was there all the time. I was thus, confined to the very small boxroom, where you would have a job to swing a cat, while his room remained big and unoccupied. Mrs P also had a rule that she locked the front door when she and her husband went to bed at 11 pm and we had no keys to get in. One night, air steward John, a nice guy, and I went to the pub for a drink. We rushed back, but unfortunately, though we desperately tried, we didn't get home until ten minutes after eleven.

John, after looking at his watch, told me that we were locked out and that we would have to sleep in the car. Me, sleeping in the car with a warm bed inside? Perish the thought! I was having none of it and rapped frantically on that front door until an annoyed-looking husband with sleep in his eyes reluctantly opened the door and let us both into our beds. Neither he nor we uttered one word.

On another occasion, a very peculiar time, the landlady, at about 5 pm, kept repeatedly telling me that she was going to visit her daughter in hospital at seven that evening. I, of course, wished her daughter a speedy recovery but I could not fathom why she then continued telling me about her daughter, over and over again. The reason soon came out. When the landlady realised, she would evidently have to spell it out, she wanted me out of the house while she was at the hospital—in other words, she didn't trust any of her lodgers to be left unsupervised in her house! Well, that was the final straw. I decided then that I needed to leave that small box room and Mrs P, and soon.

Leaving Mrs Ps comfortable abode did result in my sleeping in a few rough places! One, I remember in particular, I was pleased to get until, while sleeping in a bedroom with three single beds in the room a not so well-dressed man, stinking of alcohol, jumped into one of the spare beds at around midnight. I quickly realised, then, that it wasn't the room that I had rented, but only the bed—a little bit too risky for me, to my mind! Eventually, after trying a few grotty rented properties, I managed to find a place long term, one that I could call home, and which would give me a more relaxed life.

I did, though, sleep in the car on one occasion, waking up freezing cold at four in the morning.

British Airways put all new aircraft engineer entrants into the company's workshops, which was standard practice. Nobody wanted to work straight days in the workshops on basic money: instead, everyone wanted to do shift work on aircraft maintenance but, as a new starter, one had no choice, the short straw, so I was pretty hard up with no shift-pay. That said, after six months, British Airways would let you go on a list called the Central Register, to escape.

In the workshops, I was overhauling powered flight control units of VC10 aircraft. These were hydraulic units that worked the 'spoilers' (effectively, air brakes) on the aircraft. One incident that kept happening to others, funny but not funny when it happened to you, often occurred when the control unit had to be built and then tested in the hydraulic rig-room.

The process involved pressurising a servo valve from two separate hydraulic sources, one being a hand pump, the other being a hydraulic rig that produced a pressure of three thousand pounds per square inch. If pressure from the hand pump was slightly lost, that would allow the shuttle valve to shift too far in one direction—and red hydraulic fluid would spray onto the walls and windows of the test room, with the guy in there shouting while dyeing his clothes red for the seconds it took him to switch the bloody machine off! What a mess it made, but if it wasn't your mistake and you were outside watching through the window, it was funny, and of course, there was then a lot of cleaning up to do.

Anyway, back to adding my name to the Central Register. I asked to go into the Concorde hangar as Concorde had now been 'sold', so to speak, and was being operated by British Airways. Having been on the register for a few months, I decided to visit the Superintendent of the Concorde Fleet of aircraft. When I met him, I told him that I had worked for British Aircraft Corporation and that I had a lot of experience on the Concorde. I was amazed when he told me that I would have to have worked on VC10 aircraft to get onto Concorde at British Airways, but he said, "Let me look at where you are on the register," which he did; then, he told me I was in the queue estimating it would be about three months, but that he would put a mark by my name and look out for my name when my turn came up. Well, slightly disappointed, I went back to the workshop.

I'd not been working more than an hour when the foreman told me to report straightaway to Chris Hayman, who was responsible for the American aircraft fleet. I went to Mr Hayman's office, where he immediately asked me which shift would I'd like to go on. I thanked Mr Hayman for his kind offer but told him I had a lot of experience on Concorde and that I wanted to continue to work on that aircraft. Mr Hayman immediately said one sentence to me which changed everything, and this was it (and I quote): "You won't get a Type Licence on the Concorde!" He was right, for the American aircraft consisted of the Boeing 707, one of the first jet airliners, but one that you could get a Type Licence on. This made you particularly valuable as, in reality, you could take responsibility and sign off the whole aircraft no matter what airline it belonged to. There was no such licence that you could get, ever, on the Concorde: so, in one sentence, he had me. The very next week, I joined the night-shift on Boeing 707 aircraft, and of course, my pay was very good on night-shift.

After moving from the engineering workshops, I soon got married to a Yorkshire lass and managed to sell my house in Bristol and buy a house in Northallerton. The night-shift pattern of seven days on three or four days off suited the long distance to home in Yorkshire, and also, my mother and stepfather lived in Northallerton, too, which was how I met my first wife. Eventually, the journey to and fro got to me, so my wife and I bought a house in Harlington, right on the London-to-Bath Road, just across the road from one of the runways at Heathrow Airport. Unfortunately, when I viewed the house, I didn't realise this and just thought I had only to deal with noise from the Bath Road traffic, and when I viewed it was quiet, I thought the area was fairly quiet: what I had not been told about and had missed, was the fact that occasionally, maybe 40 times a year, if the wind changed direction, the landing runway also changed, and then my little bay windowed-semi was right under the flight path to the main aircraft landing runway.

There were many early mornings, normally around five a.m. and even some nights, when the aircraft coming into land would appear to be on a collision course for my house, flying directly over my roof only to touch down immediately after crossing the road that was outside my lounge bay window! In fact, when they flew over my back garden, the sky went dark, and I think, with a ladder, I could have done some maintenance on the undercarriage—I kid you not, the aircraft were that close.

The area was so affected by aircraft that the council gave everyone a grant for Secondary Window Glazing.

The noisiest one, and by chance, the one I now worked on every night and was licenced on, was the Boeing 707. I now know why it was called the whistling giant: the whistling noise from the four jet engines abruptly woke me up many times from my deep sleep as this giant flew right over my bedroom whistling as it flew over!

That said, I spent many happy years working for British Airways at Heathrow and joining American aircraft, working on the Boeing 707. The only downside of that was that I was working seven days on, three off, seven on four off and working permanent nights. As a young guy, nightshifts were hard, and one does look back and think, *how did I ever endure that?*

After one's last night-shift, on going to bed, your body wanted at least eight hours sleep, OK while on shift; but after the last night, if you spent the day in bed you would never sleep that night. So, instead, the only thing that you could do was to get into bed as normal and force oneself out again, feeling like crap, just four hours later. Then, you were likely to get some sleep that night but, in reality, the body could not readjust to a normal sleep pattern in the short number of days off between shift patterns, so one would be wide awake.

Worse, I would always be hungry at about three a.m., because that was normal dinner time when working nights. I only managed to get a good night's sleep the night before starting my next batch of nights, and of course, then the body was upset once again at the change in sleeping pattern—and so, it went on.

Nevertheless, I got very good at so-called 'Major Maintenance' on Boeings, first the 707 and then the Boeing 737. There were a bit of bad feelings when I asked to move from the Boeing 707 hangar over to the Boeing 737, Trident and BAC1–11 hangar, but it did allow me to acquire type licences on both Boeing 707 and Boeing 737, so I was now a licenced aircraft engineer. I knew both aircrafts well, but, on the way to gaining my licences, I had to become familiar with and work on the old 'Trident' series of aircraft and BAC 1–11s, too. Unfortunately, I could not avoid them!

One interesting point was, to get your Type Licence, you had to do an oral exam with the nice CAA surveyor. He knew his stuff, so you had to do your homework.

For example, you would be asked where the aircraft corroded which was normally under the toilets (urine is very corrosive) and how you remove the fin.

I had to do an oral exam for my Type Licence on the Boeing 707 and later, after a lot of experience on the Boeing 737, another oral had to be passed, which I will explain a little more in the later chapter.

I eventually became a certifying lead tradesman, a role that offered additional responsibilities, at Heathrow, and at times, I was asked to take on the role of supervisor. The company was crafty, though. Knowing that the engineering union's rule was that if someone remained in a supervisory role 'temporarily' for three months, there was evidently a requirement for an extra permanent supervisor, a vacancy did exist which should be filled permanently. But the company always managed to put you back down to your old job just before the three months were reached!

One day, though, while I was in that supervisory role, I was told to go to Hangar 5, a dark, remote hangar at Heathrow, and look in the freight hold of a Boeing 707, because the pressurisation dump-valve needed to be replaced. I went over, looked at the registration of the aircraft and looked in the freight hold. The hangar was dark and after looking at the job, I went back to base and found one of my team, Adrian, and asked him to change the valve when it arrived in the store.

Adrian then went over to Hangar 5 and started changing the valve. About an hour later, I went over to see how Adrian was getting on. To my shock and horror, I noticed that although the 707 was exactly in the same position, there was something very different about the aircraft: the BA colours were the same but, oops, not the registration! How embarrassing! The aircraft handlers had moved the Boeing 707 that I had inspected and replaced it with another 707. Aircraft handlers did this frequently, and it was very annoying for the engineers. I had to eat humble pie with Adrian as I told him to refit the valve again, as we were removing it from the wrong aircraft. He was not too pleased, but he didn't hold a grudge. That incident did teach me to check the registrations more than once from that day on, but in my defence, it was like a magic show, with one aircraft replacing the other at the flick of a magician's wand.

I then managed to 'escape' from Heathrow to a subsidiary of British Airways, 'British Airtours'. This was a small operation that flew charter flights to holiday destinations from a nice little airport called Gatwick. Joining Airtours was touch-and-go as, while I had passed the interview and been offered the job, there was rivalry between Heathrow and Gatwick. Another manager at Heathrow was really bitter at releasing me, but eventually, I was allowed to go. There were hard feelings—unfortunately, I had to stay on British Airways' payroll and thus could not enjoy the extra number of days holiday the British Airtours' engineers enjoyed.

Because British Airtours was a summer airline, the original staff had signed a contract that they would not take their holidays in the summer season when the airline was busy, as a reward for that the staff got almost double the annual leave. Alas, new staff like me continued with the British Airways' annual leave.

The time I spent working for British Airtours was a great time, and the director of this small company seemed to know all of us by name—so there was no hiding anymore. He would ask me directly how a certain job or repair was getting on, and I was soon promoted to a supervisory role. I had a team of engineers to look after.

The major check was extensive sometimes, taking many weeks as the aircraft was extensively taken apart and put back together and to give us variety. After every check, the supervisors and men would move from one area or zone to another, i.e., this time, we might be taking the tail to bits or be stripping the left wing, but the area none of us liked was the fuselage, because everything had to come out—seats, floors, toilets, galleys—in fact, the inside of the aircraft became just a structural tube with floor beams and stringers and longerons. The thing looked nothing like a Boeing at all.

We had a limited time to finish these major checks and, of course, some aircraft of course had more corrosion than others. There was also one little nasty problem that occurred when we jacked up a Boeing 737 on the first day of our

Corrosion Prevention and Control Program, prior to stripping down the aircraft. The culprit was a copper-tipped galley drain mast. The sink wastewater from the forward galley drains to the atmosphere while the aircraft is in flight and the 'drain mast' is heated to stop the wastewater turning to a block of ice in the subzero temperatures of flight, which could break off, and damage the aircraft. Or block the drain.

The problem was that, with the aircraft on its wheels, the mast was near the ground out of harm's way, but when we jacked up the aircraft, the mast was then just at the height of the middle of your forehead—and its sharp point was almost invisible, so an unwary individual could easily walk into it and sustain a severely cut forehead, necessitating a visit to A&E at the local hospital for stitches!

After witnessing this more than twice, I made it my mission, after the aircraft was jacked, either to find and fit the special protector or, if I couldn't find that, which was normally the case, I would find some tape and foam to use as a shield—no more stitches on foreheads on my watch!

As we got close to the finish time of the job, Darren, our superintendent, would call the supervisors in for a get-together to discuss progress. A completion time would be suggested, and every supervisor would be asked if he could make that date; normally, if we were close, we could make that a date, provided that we planned the necessary overtime. Well, I had a plan for working my team's shift, which was normally eight hours. Our finish time would normally be 6 pm, so I would ask the guys to do overtime until 10 pm—but the plan was that the lads would voluntarily give up their tea breaks and work through, so that we could instead leave at 8:30 but still be paid until 10 pm. This worked so well, and I always managed to get my jobs and area finished on time!

There was a problem, though. Embarrassing, really, once word got out. Everybody wanted to come onto my team when we did overtime, and it was a little embarrassing when another supervisor wondered why his men were not keen to do overtime on the tail of the aircraft with him but instead, volunteered to move to my area (i.e. the wings) at six for overtime with me!

One night, unexpectedly, another supervisor, Tom, stayed late with his team. Whispers were rife about what was going to happen when Phil's team packed up as 8:30 approached. My credibility was at stake, so I told the guys I was in charge of them, and the agreement between us would stand. When the time had come to go, I informed Tom that we were off.

He did not know what to do, but I pointed out that his men, like mine, hadn't taken their breaks, and performance had been unimpaired. We all went home—apart from Tom, who, I think, feeling uneasy, still left at 10 pm. Well, we were getting the aircraft out serviceable, time after time, so morale was high, and it was a good job well done.

Superintendent, Darren, of course, soon got wise to our *modus operandi* and summoned me to his office. The conversation centred on why everyone wanted to work with me on overtime: and he then came out with it—he asked why we only worked until 8:30 but were paid till 10. I replied, "Do we not finish the major check and get the aircraft out on time?" His reply was short and sharp, "Point taken," and that was the end of that conversation. I knew, as Darren knew, an aircraft even a day late out of the hangar and unable to go into service cost the company megabucks.

I respected Darren. He wasn't stupid and, like us, he had a bit of history. I had heard the story of Darren, out running the engines of a Boeing 707 but not realising that the jet blast from the engines was going into the staff car park; or that, when he ran the 707s engines at full thrust, a number of cars ended up upside down in the car park! So we were out of the same mould, he had his moments too, even before getting to superintendent, for he was only human too and I have to thank him, as he had been instrumental in my promotion to supervisor.

The closest I got to his car park event was years later, when I was running an aircraft not far from the cargo compound, where a large number of the aluminium pallets—that is, the large, shaped boxes that passengers' luggage is packed into—were stacked. The compound, to be honest, was quite a long way away from the jet pipes of the Boeing 737 engines, but the pallets were empty at the time, and my engineer on the ground headset told me, while I had had the engines at full thrust, the boxes in the cargo pound were hovering like flying carpets and, of course, while they were neatly stacked before I throttled up, they certainly weren't neatly stacked when I throttled down!

A van pulled up near the front steps and two angry, bemused loaders got out, and I was summoned from the cockpit so that they could tell me that I had messed up their compound! Of course, there was nothing I could do to make amends, so I replied, "Sorry guys, but that's life, isn't it?" I think from the look on their faces, they probably thought I was a bit deranged, but nevertheless, they drove away, and nothing more was said.

British Airtours had some great characters amongst its staff. I will always remember Sam Roper, an old avionic supervisor. He was so funny. One day, he told me he had been called into the office, and they had asked him if he was part of the problem or there to help. Then, there was Alex who, when we attended one of our progress meetings was asked, as the rest of we supervisors were, if he could confirm a definite date to finish an aircraft. He would always answer "Yes, no problem."

We would all look at him with amazement as we knew full well that he was well behind and had not a snowball's chance in hell of his team finishing his area by that date, no matter how much overtime he did: and outside the meetings, when I asked him why he had said what he said, he replied, "But Phil, I told them what they wanted to hear," and sure enough, his zone would be unable to finish as ours did, on the said day.

I remember well, on one occasion, I was asked to come in on a Sunday to set up the engine throttles, then take the aircraft outside, adjust the thrusts and check that the engines were synchronised. 'Trimming' the engines, we called it. I was told that Alex would be doing and completing undercarriage retractions on the Saturday. On the Saturday afternoon, I got a telephone call asking me if I could come in a day early without my team to help Alex as he couldn't get the nose landing gear to retract. Whenever the operating lever was moved to the 'gear up' position, the nose gear would start to unlock but stall, failing miserably, and the landing gear would stay locked down. When I arrived, I asked Alex what he had changed. "Bloody everything," he replied. He *was* stressed!

Alex's men had replaced a lot of hydraulic parts inside the undercarriage bay. Well, I had always remembered what my father said—though Dad was not an engineer, he was an office worker—but Dad always said, "Son, if it was working yesterday and has just packed up, it can't be serious." Well, using his philosophy, if the aircraft flew in with everything working, what had been changed? The main suspect had to be the freshly rebuilt undercarriages.

Well, British Airtours had sent the main and nose undercarriages to a new company for overhaul so each of the landing gears had been overhauled: but while the main undercarriages worked, the nosewheel gear did not. With a colleague on the flight deck operating the landing-gear selector, I watched the little nose gear unlock jack, ram, trying to retract and thus trying to unlock a component known as the over-centre link. This small hydraulic actuator is intended to 'break' the link just before the main nose gear retract actuator retracts the gear.

I noticed that before this poor little lock actuator could fully pressurise and break the over-centre link, the main actuator pressurised with hydraulic fluid and started trying to move the gear, overpowering the little jack and slamming the moving link closed again and jamming the lot: stalemate! No nose gear retraction and the hydraulic actuators fighting each other! So, I had a plan and got a trusty fifty-pence-piece from my pocket and asked one of my lads to get me a broom. It was a trick that I had tried before.

With all hydraulics off, and my guy on the broom, we pushed against the springs on the over-centre link with the broom handle, and while springs were unloaded, I slipped my fifty pence in the shimmed gap in the centre of the over-centre link. I then told the man in the cockpit to switch on the hydraulics. We stood well clear, selected the gear to up and, sure enough, the little jack now with less distance to travel, unlocked or broke, as we would say, the over-centre link as intended, before the main retraction jack pressurised, and up went the gear! As the gear retracted, of course, the fifty pence piece fell on the floor—but we now knew why the gear wouldn't retract. It was a simple problem; the new company had not shimmed the over-centre link correctly on the jig during the overhaul.

Well, the superintendent on duty (we nicknamed him the man from Burton's as he was always immaculately dressed and looked as though he had just come out of the Burton's the tailor's shop window, a bit like my mate Ben, always immaculate, if you recall from earlier) now wanted Alex to remove all the new hydraulic parts and put all the old hydraulic parts back. *Well, knowing Alex, best of luck with that*, I thought!

British Airtours were eager for me to work on their Tristar aircraft, too, and sent me on the eight-week course at the training school at Heathrow.

I wasn't back more than a day after the course before I was asked if I could get a team together to do what we call a 'Ghoster', that is, working all day and all night in order to finish the job on the aircraft, because the aircraft was scheduled to fly to Florida at eleven the next morning.

The job was to change the Number One engine, the left engine, on a Lockheed 'Tristar', a very big aircraft. I got my team together, which included big Karl, an ex-Royal Navy man. He was huge, and we had been asked to have a young lad with us for work experience; he would be coming in the next morning.

Well, it did take us all afternoon, then all night until early next morning, to remove the old engine and fit the new and finish the engine change. It was a big job. We were at the stage where the new engine was fitted, so we were ready to start the engine, check for leaks and check that everything worked properly. The young schoolboy, on his air experience, joined us, and we ordered a tug with towbar to come to the hangar to push the aircraft out.

Everyone was squabbling about who would help me in the cockpit as we prepared for the engine run. The tug came, and the aircraft was pushed, and now, it sat outside Airtours' Hangar 4. The aircraft steps were fitted to the right-hand service door, and Karl plugged into the ground headset socket on the nose landing gear, so that he could communicate with me in the cockpit. The wheels were chocked, and I climbed the steps and entered the cockpit but, after all the squabbling, I am not sure what happened, because suddenly, the steps were removed, and when I looked around, there was only me and the young work experience lad in the cockpit.

That meant I had to operate three panels including the flight engineer's panel *and* the engine-start panel alone—a bit of a stretch. What I knew we had *not* done for time reasons was drain the inhibiting oil, with which the fuel control unit (FCU), was filled while the engine had been in storage. There was not much oil normally in the FCU, so normally, that wouldn't be a problem—but we would find out differently today!

Just my luck, too; at 8:30 am, just when we were about to start up, the offices above Hangar 4 were filling up with men and women about to start their day's work and, of course, they saw a little bit of entertainment outside, so the office windows were now like a spectators' gallery at the Grand National. Well, I told the lad to take a seat as, sadly, he couldn't help me with the knobs and switches on the flight deck (as the cockpit is also known). As the steps were now gone, I resigned to the fact that I was on my own, so I told Karl over the headset intercom that I was going to start the Auxiliary Power Unit (APU).

The Auxiliary Power Unit is a static jet engine located in the tail of the aircraft. Once running, it provides electrics from a generator and also pneumatic air that can be used to run the air conditioning, and more importantly, allows the aircraft mainly when away from base to start its own engines via an air starter fitted to each engine.

With the APU up to self-sustaining speed and able to run the electrics and supply pneumatic air to the starter, I told Karl I would 'dry-cycle' the engine—in other words, spin it with the air starter without putting the fuel in as a first step of the test. I spun the engine and everything was good so far; the lads told Karl, then me, through the intercom, that there was no sign of oil leaks or other problems, and the oil pressure was good, so I told Karl this time, I would let the fuel into the burners and start up Number One engine.

I spun the huge RB211 engine on the air starter, and as the compressor RPM reached 25 percent, I lifted the fuel shut-off start lever to let in the fuel. I heard the 'poof' when the igniters lit the fuel as it sprayed into the combustion chambers, and the exhaust gas temperature started to rise. I asked Karl how it looked, and he replied, "Plenty of smoke. Plenty of smoke." I then noticed the EGT was rising but the RPM was falling—not what I wanted to see—so, I shut off the fuel lever off but left the starter spinning the engine, so that the engine could cool and, it was to be hoped, clear the smoke. I asked Karl what was happening. "Lots of smoke. Lots of smoke," he replied.

I could now see the smoke in front of the aircraft filling up the hangar as the wind was blowing it in. With the engine still spinning at 25% RPM on the compressor, I lifted the fuel shut-off lever back to the 'open' position. Number One engine exhaust gas temperature (EGT) started to rise again, but once again, the engine wasn't running properly—in other words, it wasn't reaching self-sustaining speed, what we call a 'hung start'. Karl was still calling out, "Lots of smoke," so I once again shut off the fuel.

I was now starting to sweat, and especially as we had an audience including the management, the EGT started dropping and the engine still spun, with me now cooling everything again; and the windows of the hangar by now were like a football stadium. I think everyone in the office was enjoying the smoky spectacle, or were they worried that Number One engine was going to blow up? The spectators were certainly making me nervous! No shortage of witnesses if I buggered this up!

I knew what the problem was. It was a simple one: the engine was trying to burn off the inhibiting oil from the fuel control unit. There was evidently a lot more in the fuel system than I thought, and *that* was what was causing the smoke. With the engine sufficiently cooled, I gave it another go, reopened the fuel shut-off valve, and *this* time, the RPM and EGT were rising together steadily. The engine was accelerating as it should to self-sustaining speed, the temperatures and RPMs looked good; the engine was now running and sounding as it should— nice and sweetly. I did all the specified checks, making sure the engine could supply the air conditioning and anti-ice systems. Karl confirmed that the grey smoke had ceased, and it was also starting to clear from inside Hangar 4. Mission accomplished! The Tristar, after I had completed the Flight Log, was ready for the eleven o'clock service to Miami, Florida.

What I had forgotten, and this is the funny part of the story, was that Hangar 4 was equipped with a state-of-the-art fire detection and extinguishing system. There were smoke detectors all over the hangar. In every corner and also midway down the hangar, there were massive 'Fire Extinguishing Foam Cannons' that, with the help of a massive diesel engine and high-pressure foam pump located in its own purpose-built building, once set off and started, were capable of firing foam from each cannon with such a pressure that would shoot as high as the roof! The fire control had activated inadvertently on occasion previously, and I had seen pictures of the remnants of two-foot-deep fire-retardant foam on the floor of the hangar. As, on this occasion, the aircraft was just outside the hangar doors, it was safe, but how lucky were we that the fire system hadn't sensed the smoke wafting in and set off the Fire Canons?

Of course, it was just as well that only after the event, over a cup of tea, we even thought of this occurring. It certainly would have given the spectators in the office windows something to talk about, and I would never have lived it down. We lived to fight another day, eh?

On one other nerve-racking day, we had a Boeing 737 in the hangar for a minor check, and we had come to the stage of de-jacking the aircraft—in other words, lowering the aircraft back onto the ground from its jacked-up position. There were two huge main jacks, each jack positioned between the fuselage and the engine to jack up the wings and a smaller jack that fitted to a jacking pad just rear of and on the right side of the nose landing gear: but this position was not for jacking up the aircraft, rather, the ram of the jack had to be about half an inch of the jacking pad.

The small jack on the front was not a lifting jack but just there, in case the aircraft didn't jack up level on the main jacks, i.e., the two main jacks and the tail jack, so the man on the front steady jack, if you like, kept a clearance of an inch or two between the steady and the jacking pad bolted on to the side of the fuselage.

The last lifting jack, with the two main jacks underneath the wings, was a tall one that extended upwards to a jacking pad that was bolted to the aircraft's tail. This also was a steadying jack that was not used to lift the aircraft but more to steady it fore and aft. The jacks, except for the nose jack, were hydraulic and operated by the hangar pneumatic air lines.

Well, that said, the engineers under the supervision of my colleague, Jack, were letting the aircraft down. I was just watching the operation, keeping out of the way. Willy Spencer was manning the nose gear jack. Suddenly, as we lowered all jacks, there was a shout from the guys operating the starboard main jack, a huge jack with a big diameter ram. Strong, it had to be, as it was required at times to hold the aircraft high in the air for weeks or months on end with all of us working on it.

Apart from the jacks having a hydraulic ram for safety, the rams were threaded on the outside, and there was a big ring nut that could be wound up or down to physically lock the jack in any position, making it safe while the aircraft was lifted off the ground. Anyway, all the jack safety nuts were released. Jack blew his whistle, and the hydraulic valves on all the jacks were opened slowly, letting the rams retract into their cylinders. Everything seemed to be going well. The aircraft gently descended towards the concrete hangar floor, and it was about two feet from wheel to floor, still jacked up, when one of the guys shouted from the right starboard big jack, "Our jack has jammed; it isn't moving!"

Well, at that point, Jack and I noticed that the skin on the top of the fuselage had become wrinkled, and the Automatic Direction Finder (ADF) antenna aerial, which consisted of a wire rope attached from the fin to halfway along the top of the fuselage and normally taught, was like a saggy washing line. I could see that Jack was starting to panic, worried, and speechless, so before Jack had a heart attack, I told all the men on the jacks to stop where they were and that we were no longer jacking down but instead going to jack back up. I then heard the chuff, chuff, chuff of the air valves on the main jacks lifting the aeroplane. To my— and especially Jack's—relief, the wrinkles disappeared from the top of the fuselage, and once again, the ADF antenna became as tight as a guitar string.

With panic over, now was the time for investigation, and it didn't take us long to realise that the right-hand jack had not jammed but had instead, without weight on it, stopped. Willy Spencer on the nose must have had a daydreaming moment: instead of looking at what he was doing, he had allowed his nose jack not to keep a gap and follow the aircraft down as he was instructed, but instead, most of the weight of the aircraft was being taken on this small jack. This was the reason for the fuselage bending, in reality, causing the starboard main lifting jack to stop retracting, and why would it? There was no aircraft weight on it anymore! After that undesirable experience, the moral of the story was clear: choose your men carefully on important tasks like on the jacks, and keep the sleepy ones well away.

Sadly, from that experience, I learnt that good selection of men was also important when you were moving the aircraft in or out of the hangar. We had a diesel tug which we connected via a towbar to the nose leg of the aircraft. A man was positioned on each wingtip and the tail, and each man had a whistle, the simple plan being, that the tug would push or pull the aircraft in or out of the hangar, and the men with the whistles would signal by a blast whenever there was a danger of any part of the aircraft contacting any part of the hangar stopping the tug. Inside the aircraft cockpit, another man was on the brakes, in case the tow bar snapped. Simple, eh? Well, that's what I thought—that was, until there was a crunch and a belated shout after the port wingtip had smashed itself up on the hangar door, while your man with the whistle in his hand yet unblown, was in a dream as the wing he was tasked with watching embedded itself in the hangar door. Of course, now the finished aircraft was now broken, the wing now in need of repair.

I was lucky in my supervisory role as it never happened to me, but that said, I did see it happen many times, and from experience seeing it happen, I did select my watchmen carefully. Nonetheless, it still seemed to happen regularly to other supervisors at the airport—amazing!

I remember once being asked again to come in on overtime to adjust engine controls, setting them up and making sure that the engines throttled up together, developing the same power at the same time. I drove in, and as I parked my car outside the hangar, I noticed that the guys were moving the aircraft. It looked nice, and complete, after having been worked on for a month in the hangar. Now, they were backing the aircraft on to the engine silencer pipes for me to do the engine run: *good time*, I thought, *to have a chat with Matt Smith, the foreman.* While we were in conversation over a nice cup of tea, one of the guys came into the office to spoil our night and to tell us they had bashed one of the flight surfaces—the port aileron—into a pair of high passenger steps! Unbelievable. A new aircraft, so to speak, and damaged already.

On another occasion, in the morning, I had gone in to start my shift, and I passed one of our Boeing 747 jumbo jets: I did a 'second take' because it was looking very strange. It was parked on a remote stand, but I noticed the nose of the Jumbo was almost touching the ground. Very strange, not something you see every day, or want to see again. When I got to work, I found out the sad details, and someone was in deep trouble. The engineers on night-shift had been asked to test the undercarriage function. To do that safely, there was, on each undercarriage leg, a hole of about an inch or more in diameter in the over-centre lock link. Remember, from previously, it's the over-centre link that locks the undercarriage down.

As you may recall, we talked about that link on the Boeing 737. In this case, the purpose of this hole is to allow insertion of locking pins on every landing gear set, and then you could happily, though still nervously, go into the cockpit, switch on the hydraulics and select the landing gear lever to 'up', and the gear doors would open, but the gear would not retract as they would in flight because each gear would be physically locked by the pins. This allowed the undercarriage doors to be tested with no worries of anything more sinister happening (like the landing gear retracting under the weight of the aircraft)!

Well, back to our funny-looking Jumbo that looked as though it was taking a bow. The engineer, on this occasion had had five landing gears to lock physically but, for some reason, there were only three locking pins available in the stores. The others were missing: so, he came up with a shortcut to get the job completed and used in the past.

Because some landing gears worked from a 'green' hydraulic system and some from a 'yellow' system, the idea was to use the locking pins on the three gears that worked on one hydraulic system to pressurise *those* gears but leave the other gears on the other hydraulic system depressurised and later swap over the process in other words do the gears in isolation. Well, I am sure you've guessed it—very risky, he got the match between the landing gears and the hydraulic systems wrong.

I am pretty sure I would have if I had foolishly tried that, so when he switched on the hydraulics and selected 'up' on the gear, to his distress, and maybe a time for wishing he had brown trousers, the unlocked gears started to retract. The nose started to go down, the two main gears tried to retract, the engineer on feeling that sinking feeling in the cockpit then panicked and moved the landing gear lever back to the down position, but the poor old hydraulic rams couldn't lift that heavy aircraft from an angle: so, instead of lifting the Jumbo, every ram on those gears bent like a banana—a very expensive mistake!

Of course, at the enquiry, when the people on the other side of the table asked him where he found that technique in the maintenance manual, there was no technique. Telling them the stores did not have the required number of undercarriage pins did not help him, sadly.

A difficult position to be put in, but for me you get the pins, or you can't do the job.

On yet another occasion, one of the engineers on the ramp was 'departing' (supervising the departure of) a 'DC10' while having his headset plugged-in and talking to the flight crew on the flight deck. He unplugged his headset after the aircraft had been pushed back from its stand, and the aircraft took off for New York. Unfortunately, the engineer this time, before unplugging his headset, forgot to remove the nose gear undercarriage pin. This pin was always fitted through the over-centre link, while the aircraft was on the ground to stop the nose gear retracting accidentally, while the 'tug' pushed the DC10 from one place to another—most often, back from its stand after having been loaded prior to departure.

The crew had started the engines, and the tug and towbar had been disconnected, the ground engineer disconnecting his headset and moving clear. Before doing that, he should have removed the pin and shown the pin to the flight crew which ought to have been acknowledged by them looking from the cockpit window, to see the pin, with its red 'Remove Before Flight' flag being waved at them.

Not only did the engineer forget to remove the pin *and* wave it towards the cockpit, but the flight crew also omitted to look to see him holding it towards them, in his hand! The DC10 took off, full of fuel, the captain selected gear up, the main gear doors opened as did the nose gear doors, the main gears retracted into the aircraft and the main doors closed—but the nose landing gear did not retract because it still had the locking pin inserted. The DC10 couldn't go to the states but instead had to fly around and dump fuel over the sea until it was light enough to land back at Gatwick: another very costly, simple mistake with thousands of pounds worth of fuel dumped over the sea!

The engineering director pushed for the poor engineer to be sacked but luckily that didn't happen.

Chapter Five
Another New Job

After many more years, during which I worked for the charter airline British Airtours, British Airways bought British Caledonian Airways. This meant that British Airtours would be lost in the combination, so I was now working for British Airways again. Not long after the merger, there was an accident when a Boeing 737, not one of ours, flying short hops between the Hawaiian Islands, you may recall it, lost most of its 'roof' (the top of its fuselage) from the cockpit at the front rearwards. The pilot, praised by the passengers as a hero, managed to land the aircraft safely, but sadly, one cabin crew member got blown out and lost her life. Once on the ground, it looked like a convertible with the hood down.

And from that day, everything changed for us in major maintenance on aircraft as the aircraft structure had failed because of cracks and corrosion as this particular aircraft did short flights being pressurised and then depressurised the fuselage blown up and deflated each flight like a balloon, stretching the cabin then retracting the cabin, which caused fatigue on the metal skin of the aircraft.

After many international meetings, it was decided by the authorities that from that accident, all airlines would be required to do greater in-depth inspections when they did any major overhauls on commercial airliners.

As a consequence, engineers us had to go much deeper with their maintenance, and the rule was that we had to get access every part of the aircraft structure so that it could be inspected visually, using a mirror and torch. All ageing aircraft came under this philosophy, the Corrosion Control and Prevention Program was born. Well, we were now tasked to look at a structure such that in places, we had never had to look at before; and when we found some parts cracked or corroded, they were normally areas never looked at before, so we had to dig out drawings to get part numbers, so as to order parts that we had never ordered before. Worse, when they arrived, we found that they were such structural parts as it was likely that they had been fitted during manufacture—meaning that they had been fitted in a certain order and would now be absolute pigs to replace without stripping down other parts for access. We would have difficulty in drilling-out those parts, necessitating removal of other parts of the structure before we could get access.

Well, of course, this was the first time any such extensive major checks would have been done on any aircraft in the fleet, so we had no idea what we would find or how many weeks, even months, the checks would take. Add to that the fact that some of the parts had to come off the Boeing 737 production line in Seattle as they were parts not normally asked for, and the whole activity became even more of an unknown. We heard that the parts ordering department had been told to order four of every 'strange' new part ordered by the engineers.

When I say strange, I mean a part that nobody had ever ordered before with the part number only found from viewing the drawing in the drawing library. There was one lady who let us into the drawing store who had a very boring job, I guess, just sitting at her desk, looking after us as we searched to find a structural part and its part number on its drawing—even finding the correct microfiche plate of the drawing was difficult enough.

Among many other corrosion areas towards the back of the aircraft under the rear toilet area (wee is very corrosive), there was a big floor beam fitted across the width of the fuselage. Through the floor beam ran the wire rope control cables for the flying controls—the tailplane, elevator, moving stabiliser and rudder; there were lots of electrical cables going through the beam too. Through check after check, the Design and Repair Department devised complicated repair schemes for this beam that took us weeks and weeks to incorporate, removing the corrosion and splicing in new strengthening parts that were machined in the machine shop, bolted and riveted on to this beam. Consequently, repairing the beam was taking ages. Something had to change.

After we had done three aircraft beams, I conferred with the avionic supervisor, and we asked why we could not disconnect the flight control cables, cut and splice the electrical looms going through the beam, remove the old beam, fit a new one and put everything back. We had this answer from the Design and Development Office: "We didn't think you could do that."

Changing this old corroded and cracked beam for a new one, instead of doing extensive repairs, saved us weeks, and eventually, we managed to reduce the check time from over three months to a month and a half. There were still some stupid inefficiencies, though. For example, if I was on the tail of the aircraft and wanted to remove the rudder or stabilisers, my engineers would get the lifting slings onto the control surfaces—but then, we would have to stop working until we could get a crane driver from the DC10 hangar. Naturally, they weren't in a rush to come over to us! The real problem was that our superintendent refused to send one of our maintenance workers on a crane-driving course, as it would mean extra pay in that worker's salary.

Tim, another supervisor, had a very short temper. He used to get so angry at the delay that he nearly had a heart attack each time. In contrast, I took it in my stride and sent the guys off for a tea break. It was annoying, nevertheless, that we couldn't get on with the job—but I was *not* going to have a heart attack over it!

Some in the company, Heathrow based, had decided that we were taking too long with these checks and that maybe the aircraft should be moved from Gatwick to Heathrow where—in the accountant's eyes—the Heathrow operation seemed to be more efficient than the Gatwick operation. What the accountants didn't realise was that at Heathrow, while they allocated a finish time for the aircraft in the major overhaul hangar, when that time came, the *un*finished aircraft would be moved, unfinished bits and all—with all the unfitted parts being put in a lorry and taken, with jobs left to do, to the 'casualty unit'—who were really pissed off at getting an aircraft all in bits to finish! But as far as the accountants understood, it was another budget, it was gone from the major maintenance hangar, so in their eyes, finished. It was a 'con' in reality; and, in contradiction of the practice at Heathrow, Gatwick aircraft—when finished—went to the ramp, were loaded with passengers and went flying—all complete, of course!

The apparent efficiency of the Heathrow engineering operation was a myth: credit was taken where none was due, rather like me and my crew working on the wings. If you could get all the flaps back on the aeroplane, even though only on the 'stops' on the tracks but not connected, you took all the glory for getting them up there, a bit of window-dressing really which pissed off the following shift who had to do the hard bit of connecting the flaps to the screw jacks. Naughty of us really but—we'd got the flaps on, hadn't we?

The similarity, albeit on a smaller scale, to fooling the accountants that it was cheaper and faster to do the Corrosion Prevention Control checks at Heathrow where the aircraft always left the hangar on time (yet it didn't go flying) but instead went into another hangar for three or more weeks to be finished off was undeniable!

In a desperate attempt to close down the Gatwick maintenance operation, 'Higher Management' at Heathrow decided to replace our failing superintendent with a new man from Heathrow, Dan Pullman. I had worked with Dan before. One's initial impression was that he looked like a rough diamond but instead, under that hard skin, he was a nice guy.

He came into the hangar when morale was low, as the men had not liked our previous boss: so, at this time, we were still taking about two or three months to do a check depending on how bad the aircraft was and how much the aircraft was corroded. The engineers were suspicious of this new superintendent, and one from my team told me that he had been talking about Mr Pullman in the toilets, telling others what a miserable guy he looked, only to hear the toilet flush operate in one of the toilet cubicles and from that cubicle out walked our new superintendent.

"Oh, hell," he said to me, "I am dead!"

I laughed, "I don't think so," I told him. "From my experience of Dan, though he looked like a Mexican bandit, he was probably having a quiet laugh in the toilet, hearing you talking about him."

Of course, I was right.

It was mentioned to me, via my foreman with whom I got on well (recognising and despite his sarcasm) that Dan Pullman wanted to tell the engineers via me, as I guess they knew I had a good rapport with the lads, that if we could get the next aircraft completed in a month, he would organise a party for the hangar staff. I listened to that statement and reconfirmed that statement with my foreman and, of course, I passed it on to the engineers—which, I guess, he knew I would do.

Well, human nature is such that when you have a new boss, you always give the boss a holiday period to find out what he is like and how he performs—if you like, a temporary holiday for a few months while you suss him out finding out about his character; and the engineers were sussing Dan out. Now, the offer of a party was a nice gesture: it was appreciated and morale increased. Off we went, and guess what, morale was high, and we finished the aircraft CP check within a month!

Of course, this was about our third Corrosion Prevention Check aircraft, so the parts were hopefully by now sorted and we were experienced.

It then went a bit quiet, about the party promise, which was until I reminded my foreman, and hence Dan, that the consequences of a reneged promise would be dire for them (and me, being the messenger), so true to his word, the party was arranged, and everyone was happy, and morale was high and everyone was happy with our new hangar manager, Dan Pullman. I found out through the grapevine later, though, a little twist to the story: Dan had only a £500 budget that he could claim for a party or anything else that was his expense limit, and he was dead worried that the amount would not be enough for all of us in the hangar—but his £500 was enough, because only half the hangar could attend, but it didn't matter as the nice gesture was set.

When Higher Management at Heathrow heard that we were able to get the aircraft finished in a month, of course, they made a big thing of it. We were even in the British Airways newspaper, on the front page, and Dan Pullman was a star, a beacon for a manager who could get results. I heard, though, that while at Heathrow, Dan had thumped his boss—so I suspect, now my view only, that Heathrow management had had an ulterior motive for sending him to our hangar at Gatwick and that was to 'bury' him, as being the last manager to fail to get the aircraft out before our work on the Corrosion Control and Prevention Program was to be shifted to Heathrow.

Unfortunately for the Heathrow guys, their plan had failed as Dan had performed to the contrary and was a hero. I guess these managers had to come to Gatwick with gritted teeth when they had to pose for photographs with Dan, next to our Boeing 737 finished in record time!

That was not all. The Heathrow guys did get a bit nasty with the engineers at Gatwick as well, always being jealous of our performance. Once an aircraft was finished, it normally needed a flight test with all the cost of crew, fuel and landing fees that that involved. The real reason for the test was that the elevator manual servo tab had to be set on each aircraft check, and *this* required a test flight. The test was that while in flight, the crew, as part of the test flight, had to turn off all the flight control hydraulics (those being to the ailerons, elevators and rudder) in effect and fly the aircraft manually without powered assistance to inspect the aircraft's behaviour. On switching off the hydraulics and with the servo tab now unlocked and helping to control the elevator pitch, it was not unusual for the nose of the aircraft to select a new neutral, if not set by us properly and to pitch up but, it was hoped, not too aggressively.

The elevators are normally fully hydraulic, controlled by two hydraulic systems. On the right-hand elevator, there was a little hinged servo tab (a small panel). Normally, this tab would be 'faired' with the elevator in its normal (inactive) position when the hydraulics are 'on'. A 'pass' on the flight test would result if the captain, after turning off the hydraulics, could turn the stabiliser trim wheel to correct the nose-up pitch to level flight within three turns of the big trim wheel, moving the stabiliser to a new position. Any more than three turns, and the test was a fail. Then, the engineers would have to readjust the tab, requiring another flight test and so on until the test was passed—you can see the pound signs rising for British Airways.

The Boeing 737, one of the safest aircrafts in the world, has the facility to be able to be controlled by the flight crew manually if, heaven forbid, all the main hydraulic systems were to fail. This is done by what we called 'manual reversion'—though it is a bit heavy on the pilots' muscles, like losing powered steering on your car.

There are two, red, guarded switches marked A and B and Standby Rudder. When the switch-guards are in the flat (normal) position, the A and B hydraulic systems control the ailerons, elevator, rudder and the flaps and slats. If the worst happens, the pilots can switch the two switches to the standby rudder position, and that would depressurise the ailerons and elevator. The rudder and the crew's control wheels would then operate the ailerons and elevator directly, but because the rudder is too big to be moved by the pilots manually against the aircraft's slipstream in flight, the switch position also activates a small separate standby hydraulic pump that pressurises a normally dormant hydraulic 'servo' connected to the rudder (to provide mechanical assistance).

The standby hydraulic pump would also work the leading-edge flaps, and an electric motor would put down the trailing-edge flaps for landing—ingenious— so without hydraulics, the pilot flying (one is flying, one is monitoring) could control the aircraft by manually moving the ailerons and elevator, and using this little standby pump and actuator, the rudder would move, too.

Now, the elevator servo tab, as I said earlier, is normally 'faired' so inactive (level with and not protruding from) the elevator and pressurised by the A and B hydraulics. When the hydraulics are turned off, or lost, the tab springs into the airflow and act as a servo tab to assist the pilot with moving the elevators. That keeps the aircraft level and stops it pitching up.

Well, our 'Bible' for everything we did was the aircraft maintenance manual. We had to obey its instructions at all times, and from experience, I knew that part of the adjustment range in the manual which worked to within the limits specified and, when set, this setting always satisfied the requirements of the flight test every time with no pitch up and no turns of the trim wheel. In Hangar Four, our home, so to speak, we got so good at it that my boss persuaded the British Airways flight crew that once we had set the tab, there was only need for the flight test for elevator tab function and that the aircraft could thereafter go straight into service.

My boss endeavoured to persuade the crew of a Scandinavian Airlines System (SAS) aircraft that we maintained that everything would be good on their flight test: he even told them that the engineer who set up the tab would be with them (bloody hell, that was me—only joking). You fixed it, you test it, and I wasn't even a pilot myself at this time. Well, the Scandinavian pilots and I were in the cruise, I too in the cockpit and ready to switch off the hydraulics. I could see that the crew were very nervous, the captain's finger twitching on the flight control guarded switches. "Go on, it will be OK," I said and when the switches were switched from A and B hydraulics to standby rudder the aircraft did not move from stable flight, no trim wheels needed to be turned, perfect!

From then on, it was deemed that if my team set the tab, a flight test for that alone was really not necessary. The Heathrow operation once again, news about this got to them and they had 'sour grapes'—evidently annoyed when asked by their bosses why Gatwick could set the tab, but Heathrow engineers could not, costing the airline many flight tests before Heathrow got it right—and remember, we had already stopped Heathrow from taking the CPC program from us at Gatwick. Heathrow managers then got nasty and accused us of doing something not in accordance with the maintenance manual, to set the tab. Sour grapes indeed and of course we didn't give them any advice!

We did though, sometime later at Gatwick, have a Boeing 737 that had failed the flight test with the nose pitching up beyond limits. After the aircraft landed and returned to the hangar, the engineers in the minor maintenance hangar nothing to do with us in major maintenance; had unfortunately got it wrong again, and after one failed test flight, adjusted the tab in the wrong direction. This frightened the life out of the crew even more during the next flight test as, when they turned off the hydraulics this time, the nose pitched up so abruptly that the crew said that they thought they were flying a space rocket and going into orbit!

This, to make it worse, was the same crew of the aircraft that had failed on the previous test. They were caught unexpectedly and were not pleased! The aircraft then became our property to sort out and, after reading the log and realising the mistake of the minor hangar crew, re-adjustment this time in the correct direction was made and all was well.

Chapter Six
A Second Change of Direction

I eventually went on to working on the ramp, where I got to look after the Boeings and the Tristars and the DC10s with my new teams of engineers. I did miss my old team from the hangar, but it was a good move back to quick troubleshooting and decision-making for me.

I was called out to a Tristar (a three-engine aircraft) with all its passengers on board. When the captain had tried to start the Number Three engine (the engine on the starboard or right-hand side, looking from the cockpit windscreen) during the start, the passengers had been treated to sheets of flame coming from its jet pipe, and on arriving at the aircraft, I was told they endured this spectacle on three start attempts; good start to your bucket and spade holiday, eh?

The aircraft was a 'third party' aircraft, belonging to Caledonian Airways, and British Airways Engineering was contracted to look after Caledonian aeroplanes. The company's representative was anxiously moving around the aircraft he suspected and kept saying it (HP) shaft failure, that's the biggest shaft in the engine and it connects the compressor to the turbine, one of the strongest parts of the engine.

I had never heard of such a part on a Rolls Royce engine failing, the biggest shaft in the engine, a bit like the crankshaft breaking in the engine of your car—so I was not convinced and looked for something else. When I went up the front stairs and entered the front door of the aircraft, all the passengers' faces were looking scared to death and at me, wondering if they were off on holiday—or not.

I felt a bit like Harry Potter as I was now the only solution to them going on holiday or not, but unlike Harry Potter, I didn't have a magic wand to help me, so no pressure then! I entered the cockpit. There, the captain in the normal left seat position, co-pilot next to him in the right-hand seat and the flight engineer at the engineer's panel.

I asked the captain, "What are you doing when you are starting the engine, Captain?"

"Well, Eng' (that was always our nickname to the flight crews), I am spinning the engine over on the starter, and when the RPM reaches 25 percent, I open the fuel shut-off valve to let fuel into the engine as per the check list as I have always done."

"OK," I said, "Let me have a go." I asked the flight engineer to turn the air conditioning off for a minute so that I could get maximum air pressure to the air-operated starter on the engine [that air coming from the Auxiliary Power Unit (APU) installed in the tail of the aircraft]. The APU, as you may recall from previous is a little jet engine, in reality, which supplies air for air conditioning, starting engines and for supplying electrical power.

Well, I opened the start valve, and the High-Pressure Pneumatic air fed to the starter on number 3 engine. The engine compressor started turning and the RPM started rising. I let it run to its maximum without letting the fuel in and to my surprise the RPM gauge went up to 38 percent: from experience, even on a good day with the wind behind you, I had never seen an engine air starter ever get up to more than 25 or 26 per cent, tops. The normal procedure was to open the fuel cock allowing fuel into the combustion chambers of the engine at 25 percent, but this time, I let the RPM run to its maximum 38 per cent RPM as indicated on the gauge, then opened the fuel shut-off, and the fuel was added. The jet engine lit up and accelerated to normal self-sustaining speed, and guess what? No flames shooting out of the jet pipe this time.

The captain asked me what the problem was. I told him that the RPM gauge was faulty, over-reading, and that when he let the fuel in at 25 per cent RPM, the engine speed was actually about 14 per cent RPM. Shoving the fuel in with such slow compressor revolutions per minute results in too much fuel or over-fuelling and flames shooting out of the tailpipe. I told him that the indicated 38 per cent RPM was in reality only 25 percent RPM according to his gauge.

Before I got on my radio and ordered a new gauge, the easy way to prove the fault was to swap the faulty gauge with its sister sitting right next to it on the instrument panel, as the three engine gauges were next to one another and one captive screw allows one gauge to be slid out, unplugged, and swapped for another. Of course, it was not just a gauge but a black box about a foot long with a plug on one end and a dial on the other. An over-reading gauge was proved by the swap. I ordered a gauge from the store. I got off the aircraft and all engines were started—no flames this time, and there was relief on the faces of the passengers; off on holiday, after all! Another mission accomplished. The new gauge arrived from the stores just before the aircraft left the stand, so we quickly handed it up to the crew through the door so that the flight engineer could fit it at their destination. Don't you love it when a plan comes together?

Another funny incident made me laugh but, in reality, it wasn't funny at the time, especially for Kevin, but funny for me afterwards—not at the time, though. A Boeing 737 came on to stand, and the captain wanted to speak with a Senior Airline Engineer—me, as it turned out. The captain told me that he had tried to start the APU after he had landed, standard practice on taxying to the stand, and that the Auxiliary Power Unit hadn't started—and that he had tried to start it three times. The crew left the cockpit, I sat in the captain's seat, and then Kevin, the electrician, arrived. I told him that the APU had failed to start and that the crew had tried three times. I said that in my opinion, the problem was probably the igniter, basically a spark plug but, of course, the igniter was electrical, and Kevin was the electrical expert on this.

"OK," he said, "Give me a chance to get steps up to the back, and open the APU access door, then you give it a try."

"Are you sure?" I asked. "The pilot had three attempts at starting it!"

"Yes, that will be OK," Kevin replied.

Now, the reason for my having asked "Are you sure?" was that whenever you try to start an APU, you shove a bucket of jet fuel into its combustion chamber, and every time you repeat the start, another bucket goes in—so, with my simple arithmetic, that was three buckets! A lot of fuel had gone into that little jet engine and still no start, so I suspected a swimming pool in there. The sensible thing to do would be to wait maybe 30 minutes for the fuel to evaporate.

Well, Kevin had told me to go for a start, so that is what I did. As I turned the rotary switch to start, surprise, surprise, the APU started. The exhaust gas temperature was on the increase and so was the RPM. Then, to my surprise, about twenty seconds later, the RPM was decreasing, and the APU started to run down. I was confused, racking my brains for a reason—then, a really flustered Kevin appeared behind me in the cockpit, frantically shouting, "Shut down! Shut down!"

Without my help, the APU was shutting down! The problem was that the unburnt jet fuel in the jet pipe had ignited, and flames were blowing out of that pipe rather like the flame from a plumber's blowtorch. That was until Kevin, in a panic, went to the undercarriage bay, where there was a big red APU emergency shutdown handle and a switch next to the handle to fire the APU fire extinguisher bottle, which, in this instance, would have been absolutely useless to put out burning fuel in the jet, for this was an internal fire inside the jet pipe. Better to let the APU run with flame blowing out of the jet pipe until it had used all the excess fuel and blown all the flames out, but no, Kevin didn't think but instead, panicked, and pulled the handle that shut down the APU and now, without any air blowing through, flames were licking up the aircraft's rudder, and the fire service, seeing the flames, was on its way!

Luckily, the flames lasted only about a minute, and nothing seemed damaged; luckily, too, the APU fire bottle switch had not fired the extinguishant uselessly all over the outside of the engine, so at least we didn't have an aircraft delayed while we fitted a new fire bottle! I did reflect a little later, thinking, "I did tell you, Kevin."

I mentioned earlier that there had been a Merger of British Airtours and British Caledonian. That did not go very smoothly at first from our point of view, that is, of the employees at British Airtours. We were offered a hundred pounds or thereabouts, or a drinks decanter. We had a choice of 'either or' while the British Caledonian staff were rewarded with a lumpsum payout to 'sweeten' their joining British Airways; and, worse from our point of view, most of them got a promotion as a sweetener, too, stepping over us.

It reminded me of a skinny cow eating the fat one but then staying skinny. After all, British Airways had saved their jobs in reality.

Management at British Airways (responsible, remember also responsible, for British Airtours as part of BA) did not want a repeat of the historic merger of BOAC and BEA that had taken place many years previously, where things being done gradually had created two divisions—the BEA guys and the BOAC guys in competition. So, this time, management decided to just throw us together from the start. It did cost British Airways, though, as it seemed that all the staff promotions were going to British Caledonian staff. I think the management thought that the BCAL staff were the more militant and so, wanted to make the BCAL staff feel good about joining British Airways giving them more favourable terms—but that didn't bode well for the British Airtours' guys, and to the dismay of BA's management, there was then an exodus of British Airtours' expert engineers.

This exodus helped to start British Airways' rival, 'Virgin Atlantic'. Not only did Virgin buy British Airtours' only Boeing 747 but Virgin Atlantic's entire engineering department took almost all British Airtours' engineers, who were trained on the Boeing 747 by BA, and held all the engineers' licences required by the authorities for Virgin to start an airline from day one. This was a consequence of the fact that the Airtours guys were pissed off because they had seen their expected promotions go to British Caledonian staff, and this was their revenge!

One of my friends, Mike (the same supervisor as in the nitrogen bottle breathing incident paragraph below) got the post of Chief Engineer at the newly formed Virgin Atlantic. Mike approached me with a job offer, which I declined gracefully I had many years in, but a lot of good guys went, including Karl the tall ex-navy man, who you may remember from the smoky hangar incident and who was on my team. A sad time for us: we lost a lot of highly trained engineers to Virgin.

I remember, at British Airtours, working with Mike before the merger. Mike was supervising his team of engineers. He headed a unit that had a mobile workshop and travelled around the airport, fixing the company aircraft like a hit squad for specific one off jobs. They were named the 'Maintenance Casualty Unit'. One night, I was supervising my team, and we were working on a Lockheed Tristar—in case you've forgotten, a big three-engine Jumbo type aircraft. We were doing the service check; a big check called a 'Ramp 3' check. Mike's men were looking to put right some snags, one of which was a hydraulic leak from Number Two engine bay—that was, the engine high in the air on the tail of the aircraft. I watched as one of Mike's men got a hydraulic lift platform under the Number Two engine and under the opened engine bay door.

The hydraulic fluid, 'Skydrol', is a violet-coloured phosphate 'Ester' fluid. It's not nice. We were told during our training that it wasn't poisonous but that if we drank a thimble-full, we wouldn't get to the toilet in time! Not sure who tested that one but what we had all experienced was a drop of Skydrol in the eye; that would stop you in your tracks, because you would close your eyes with the most excruciating pain, and having your eyes washed out at the medical department wasn't much better either! Also, Skydrol didn't smell nice or taste nice if you got any on your lips. In fact, you couldn't function with Skydrol in your eye. Instead, you had to be helped off the aircraft and escorted to the medical department! This was the reason for Mike's man wearing a breathing mask—for throat and eye protection.

Well, suddenly, I saw this man fall to the ground. He hadn't even got onto the platform but fell down with a crash onto the concrete hangar floor, cutting his head. I rushed over, pulled the mask off his face and called Mike, his supervisor, over. Mike told me that he intended to stop his men from working and that he was going off with his man in the ambulance to Accident and Emergency at the hospital. I told him that we had almost finished the ramp-check and that once finished, I would see if I could climb up and locate the Skydrol leak. I put on the mask and started to ascend the platform. I had just spotted the leak and then the next thing I knew, Adrian was calling out to me, "Phil, are you OK?"

I, too, was horizontal now on the platform. Luckily, I hadn't hit my head on the way down, and when I came round and recovered and my brain started working again, I did a bit of thinking—and realised that wearing a facemask connected to dry nitrogen bottles, dry air that we used for inflating tyres, was not a good idea! We breathe with every breath a mixture of about 78% nitrogen, 21% oxygen and about 1% other gases, so I was missing the important 21% oxygen I needed for my brain to function, and it didn't like it! Instant hypoxia! The doctors at the hospital must have been scratching their heads and about to get a lot of tests underway on this poor engineer, until I called Mike on his phone to tell him what had happened to me and why.

Mike told me that they had used the mask many times, I am not sure how the guys had got away with that.

We had lots of problems with the aircraft handlers moving aircraft. I experienced this again when I moved to the Gatwick Ramp, because an aircraft would arrive on stand for the night, the passengers would disembark, the engineers would start to do their ramp-check, and when they returned from having a cup of tea, lo and behold, the aircraft would have disappeared and now be parked probably in the most inhospitable area on the airport, namely the cargo area, where the wind howled and where working on the aircraft became difficult.

The reason for such moves was cost: it cost more to park an aircraft on a stand overnight than in the cargo area, but it made our job ten times harder. Relations at one time got so bitter over this that the engineers started to put a jack under the wheels of the aircraft as if they were changing a tyre. Of course, this meant that the aircraft handlers didn't dare move that aircraft!

Chapter Seven
My Start on the Road to Being a Pilot

In 1987, I realised that socially, I had become a very boring guy, doing nothing apart from working, and thus, I had to lie about my hobbies when I was filling in application forms. This was when I decided that I would have to change my life. I was always at work or thinking about work, and I had no hobbies, but I had to put something down, so I put down 'fishing' as a hobby on any form—a complete untruth, as the last time I had fished was as a boy.

My work as an aircraft engineer, though, was exciting and rewarding. Fixing problems was all-consuming with nothing outside. What should I do? It was evident that with aircraft in my blood, so to speak; flying the things instead of just fixing them was the way to go. *Unfortunately, I was too old by this time,* I thought, *to train as a commercial pilot with the expectation of gaining a job: I had missed my chance; that ship had sailed.*

However, British Airways had a private flying school associated with it in High Wycombe, at 'Booker' Aerodrome (now known as Wickham Air Park), so that was my first port of call.

I struggled with my first lessons, mainly because of not having just one instructor allocated to my training but having different instructors for various lessons—a common practice at most flying clubs. The club there used Piper PA38 aircraft, the 'Tomahawk', which always frightened me to death when I was taught to stall it and to recover. The Tomahawk, arguably, is not—from the student's point of view—an ideal aeroplane for stalling: in particular, while some aircraft used as trainers have a natural tendency towards longitudinal stability (a good thing in stall recovery) the Tomahawk, again arguably, isn't one of them.

I did have an elderly instructor, of long experience, called Gerald. I liked him. He was a nice, elderly guy and was a good teacher, but he worked only part-time, and I ended up with Dave. *Dave wasn't so good, and he stupidly put me under stress and tested me during one training flight—a bit premature*, I thought, as I had only just started my training. During our first flight, Dave presented me with a test question. "We are lost," he said, "so what should we do?" Bemused at such a question, on the first flight with him, I suggested not being serious that we should find a field big enough to land in, to which he retorted, and I quote "What? Can't you see the brickworks?"

I pointed out that I didn't live in that part of the country and that I had only just started flying. *He looked a bit dumbfounded! Not such a good instructor*, I thought. I wasn't learning to fly first and navigate next, the way in which I thought matters ought to proceed; and that was my first and last lesson with him and the end of my flying with that club.

So, the question was, where to go now? One of my colleagues at work flew a microlight aircraft, so I, with the help of my ex-wife, took interest in finding out more about that—after all, it seemed that they were cheaper and required fewer training hours to achieve award of a pilot's licence. My ex-wife did some research and found a safe microlight aircraft called the 'Shadow' and discovered that there were two schools where tuition on them was available, one in Coventry and one near York. This is where my new adventure began. The main advantage of learning to fly a microlight aircraft is that it brings private flying to the ordinary man, me, so that was the way I went.

I progressed well in my training with Brendon, my instructor. The location was a small ex-World War II strip near York called Full Sutton. In fact, it has a prison, HMP Full Sutton next to the airfield. I bought a very old motor caravan that I called 'Bertha', and my wife, three kids and I travelled from London to York on my days off.

My life has, unfortunately, never been without problems. Bertha was lovely to sleep and to relax in but she had two big problems: first, I noticed that I was getting headaches when driving her, and it took me quite a while to figure out that we were suffering the effects of carbon monoxide—poisoning—but then, when carbon monoxide was suspected, I also could not understand why opening the driver's and passenger windows, or in fact any window, seemed to make the poisoning worse. I eventually worked it out.

The wrong exhaust, one that was too short, had been fitted. In fact, one made for a Bedford Van by the previous owner, not long enough for Bertha, a Bedford Motorhome; and as a result, the fumes were permeating through the long bench seats so opening my driver's window just sucked more exhaust gas into the vehicle.

The other frustrating but less serious problem with old Bertha was that because she was so old, all the electrical power to the headlights went through the headlight switch, they didn't use relays in those days, and after the headlight switch had been 'on' for some time, it became hot and failed, and the bloody headlights started to flash at other vehicles all by themselves! We seemed to make a lot of friends without intending too, until we got a new switch.

But apart from problems with the motor caravan, I got good at this flying and was approaching my first flight without an instructor, or going 'solo' as we call it, I decided to take out a loan to buy my own Shadow aircraft at a cost of about £16,000, similar in cost to a medium-sized car at that time.

When I flew with Brendon in my new aircraft, fresh out of the factory, on the very first flight, we had a bloody engine failure, and Brendon bought the aircraft safely back down to the airstrip. After the second failure once on the ground, Brendon said to me, "How come you are so cool when the bloody engine fails, Jamesy?"

"Well," I replied, "you were flying the aircraft, Brendon!"

That said, and after the engine had failed four times, Brendon had had enough and decided that the Shadow had to go back to the aircraft factory to be sorted out. We couldn't understand why the engine had failed in different stages of flight. Of course, the bloody thing always started and behaved itself straight afterwards on the ground. It was a very strange fault.

Luckily, and by chance because they were struggling to fix this, the factory eventually found the cause—a slither of rubber from a poorly cut rubber fuel pipe that was floating up and down in the fuel pipe was being sucked up on high power, as in a vacuum cleaner, up the pipe to block the carburettor float needle, stopping the fuel and hence the engine, and then, innocently floating back down the fuel pipe under gravity and leaving no trace—like a criminal leaving the scene after the crime—allowing the engine to run perfectly well when back on the ground at low throttle settings. Very frustrating! Carburettor icing has a similar effect, in that the frozen fuel-air mixture which forms in the carburettor venturi blocks the carburettor, stops the engine, then melts away, leave no trace like a criminal leaving the scene after the crash!

Anyway, with the problem found and sorted, back to incident-free flying, or so I thought. I progressed well, and as I was getting close to going solo and completing the dual part of my training, I decided to build a trailer for the aircraft so that I could transport it around, on tow, behind Bertha. Microlight aircraft flying at that time was very affordable. I built the trailer outside, at the side of the house. My big four-wheel trailer was not beautiful, but it did the job. The wings and tail were easily removed from the Shadow, like a kit, really perfect!

The Shadow neatly tucked up inside the trailer, but once hitched up to Bertha, the combination was very long, so we had to put a 'long vehicle' sign on the trailer's rear tailgate door. Unfortunately, I didn't fit brakes to the trailer. I had looked at the law relating to brakes on trailers and, though I should have weighed the trailer, I thought that with an aircraft weighing a mere 150 kilos, the combination was within the allowable unbraked trailer weight. The loaded trailer would fall within the 'unbraked' category.

On one trip from Hounslow, where I was living at the time, to York, shortly after I started my journey, I stopped and looked around the trailer. I noticed that instead of four wheels on the trailer, there were only three! After uncoupling the trailer and a brief back-track and rerun of my route, I found that there was no sign of the missing wheel. What could I do? I had no spare wheel for the trailer, so I decided to ignore the strange look on the left-hand side and carry on until we got all the way to our destination in Yorkshire, where hopefully, I could get the trailer fixed: how funny we must have looked! I just looked straight ahead, definitely making no eye contact with other drivers, who evidently took a second look at what they thought they were seeing. That was a bit embarrassing, especially when on the motorway, with the slip-road traffic merging on my left, the side of the missing wheel and worse in slow traffic, so I definitely kept my eyes looking straight ahead, then!

Embarrassment over, we arrived in Yorkshire at Full Sutton, and while I learnt to fly with my excellent instructor, Brendon, I found a trailer maker to sort out my problems with the trailer. Unfortunately, though, on one trip with Bertha to Yorkshire with the family on board and with four wheels in tow, an over-zealous police officer pulled me over, insisting that we follow him to a weighbridge—where he found that we were slightly over the maximum permitted unbraked trailer weight, as a consequence of which, I received a court summons. I could see from his partner's face, though, that his colleague thought that pulling over a family with three children and dragging them to a weighing station to find out that we might have got the trailer's weight wrong was not what he thought policing was all about.

My brother-in-law, who worked for the Ministry of Transport (as it was then called) gave me some good advice, telling me to take pictures of the aircraft and trailer to explain my mistake—he said that the Judges love pictures, and he was right. It was, after all, a 'human error' that under 650 kilos, no trailer brakes were required, and over 650 kilos trailer brakes were required. Of course, I was fined, but the judge was lenient and as nice as he could be in dealing with my mistake.

Brendon had a little group of club members who flew the 'flexwing' aircraft at Full Sutton. Flying a flexwing aircraft is a bit like flying motorbikes all open with your face in the air stream—if you can imagine that. Many people prefer the thrill of this open cockpit flying. I often saw these members come to Brendon's little airfield after they had finished work—but even when flying conditions were perfect, I never saw them do any more than stare up at the brilliant skies and talk about going flying. Brendon told me that they always found some reason not to fly. It was evident to me that the club camaraderie was as good to them as the flying would have been!

Well, after lots of weekend trips with wife and kids up to Yorkshire and, with that, some wasted journeys because the weather didn't play ball, I finally went on my first solo flight—with Brendon watching me nervously from the ground, as I now do when my own students go solo.

After a few more solo flights, there was one session when I flew circuits. This involves taking off, flying around the airfield 'circuit pattern' and then landing: and then, you repeat the process on your own many times. One circuit I remember vividly, and I always talk about it to my students so that they can learn from my experience. The weather was perfect, with sunshine and no wind. My landings were good, and everything was easy. I was just starting to get too relaxed. I turned base leg, tracking Full Sutton Prison fence before turning onto final approach to the runway, the sixth repetitive landing, and I admit that I was a bit too relaxed.

Suddenly, on final approach, my left wing dropped sharply for no apparent reason, but evidently, the right wing had hit a thermal, i.e., an updraft of hotter air, and the aircraft, at about 200 ft above the ground, started a steep left turn, with my hand frozen on the side stick and me stunned, too. I could see in my peripheral vision the hard runway starting to disappear, apparently moving off to the right. Suddenly, a voice in my subconscious barked at me, "Well, do something, you pratt, you're going to crash!"

After hearing that, voice it was like an electric shock. I quickly came out of my dream, sprang back into life and started flying the aircraft again. That one incident early in my training taught me a lot—that being to always expect the unexpected, while flying an aeroplane and to always be prepared and you won't get caught out. I now tell my students the story and tell them that take-off and landing are the critical phases of flight, so always be prepared for the unexpected in those phases of flight.

In hindsight, I suspect that the aircraft was hit under its right wing by a rising 'dust devil', a violent updraft. Nevertheless, it was a lesson well-learnt and one I've never forgotten. I remember that after I had woken up and corrected the aircraft's approach, hoping that my instructor, Brendon, wasn't watching that particular approach, as I am sure I would have got a rollocking had he been watching! Luckily, he was oblivious to that particular landing!

It became apparent that now that I was able to fly solo and I was lucky enough to own my own microlight aircraft, travelling to an airfield much closer to home would be a better option for me, as those hundreds of miles from Sussex to Yorkshire were getting expensive and too much—especially if, after having arrived there, rain or wind stopped play. The wife and kids were not too happy either, when that was the case. So, time for a change of training location. I joined a flying club near Basingstoke where the club's chief flying instructor, Steve, agreed to supervise the rest of my flying training but that was with one proviso—that I parked my 'Shadow' well away from his 'Thruster' aircraft as he didn't want his students to think that it was a school aircraft and want to fly it instead of his Thrusters, which unfortunately, they did!

There was also one other important thing you had to worry about, and that was the owner of the airfield—Jack, a miserable man, who could take unbelievable umbrage if you spilt petrol on his field. The best weed killer for grass, unfortunately, was petrol, and to spill petrol while you refuelled with your fuel can brought on an angry Jack, who gave you one of two options—the better option was that you were given a spade to replace the spoilt turf, the other option, especially if he didn't like you, was to be asked to leave. If he chose you and your aircraft to leave his airfield, you could never return. Learning to fly became the least of your worries, as upsetting the owner—and he was easily upset—was far worse and therefore always paramount in your mind. This made flying very stressful.

The airfield, though, was, of course, closer than the one in Yorkshire, yet still a couple of hours away, especially if you had on tow a Shadow aircraft in a trailer motoring at fifty miles per hour maximum. Frustratingly, on one particular day, I did the long journey and arrived at the airfield only to find that the pins to connect the ailerons, the flaps and the elevator to the controls had been left in a pocket of my other trousers that had been in the wash! So, after having wasted that trip, when I got back home, I luckily found all the pins and clips trapped in the washing machine door seal after they had evidently fallen from my trouser pocket and rattled around during the wash. I made sure, after that waste of a trip, time and petrol, that I put all the pins back in their respective holes back in the aircraft from then on!

Chapter Eight
My Pilot's Licence Arrives

After my General Flight Test—the flying test which all students have to pass to acquire a licence—my pilot's licence eventually arrived. I was now fully licenced to fly a microlight aircraft. Unfortunately, being a very inexperienced pilot, as we all are at that stage and in the early days, navigation was not easy, as we did not have all the electronic satellite aids that we have now—and I got lost many times.

One of my worst experiences occurred when I tried to fly to Sandown in the Isle of Wight but found that the headwind was too strong, and I was running out of fuel. The 'Shadow' had only enough fuel for 2 hours flying, as a maximum, which was not much if you had a strong headwind that was effectively stopping you moving over the ground. After all, although the Shadow in the eighties was one of the faster microlights, capable of achieving about seventy miles per hour which was the normal groundspeed when flying that aircraft, a twenty-five-mile-per-hour headwind meant that the aircraft was travelling over the ground at about forty miles per hour. With a one-and-three-quarter-hour fuel quantity and a reserve, that didn't get you very far.

I watched the fuel gauge gradually getting closer to the last quarter mark, so I called Southampton Air Traffic Control (ATC) on the radio, and they gave me the frequency of HMS Daedalus, at that time a Royal Naval Air Station, at Lee-on-Solent and very close to the coast. As I had no fuel to cross the Solent to the Isle of Wight, HMS Daedalus was my only safe option—quit while ahead and ask to land at HMS Daedalus.

I was cleared to land by the controller, who had been briefed by Southampton about my serious problem, that I was short on fuel. Being unable to communicate initially with HMS Daedalus, I had hoped that its 'Stinger' missiles (I felt sure that Daedalus *had* Stinger missiles) would not be pointed at me—although, that said, after I landed an escort with what looked like very big guns, they told me to stay in the aircraft before marching me and my passenger, Len, to see the commander of the base. His tone was threatening at first as he asked me for an explanation as to why I had landed at his Royal Naval Air Station. Thankfully, his tone changed from foe to friend when I told him that I had had to land, that because of the wind aloft, I was almost out of fuel.

He then remarked that my landing was better than his student pilots flying RAF Bulldogs, which was a nice compliment.

When the fuel bowser came over to refuel our little Shadow aircraft, the refueller asked me how much fuel I wanted. I told him to fill it up—25 litres. He laughed, saying, "We wash out the bucket with more fuel than that." We all laughed. Once fuelled, we thanked, and bade farewell to, the Commanding Officer, who was curiously looking over this strange-looking aeroplane—but not before we had accepted an invitation from him to bring the aircraft back to Daedalus and show off the Shadow at his aerodrome family Open Day coming up that July!

Our little Shadow lined up on the end of that huge runway, normally used for landing bombers and huge transport planes, but now, our microlight Shadow, rolling fast and leaping into the air while using only a fraction of that huge runway. One funny thing arose from the HMS Daedalus event: when, about a week later, I got my bill from the Ministry of Defence for two thousand five hundred litres of fuel, I nearly had a heart attack! Twenty-five litres of 'Avgas' (aviation gasoline for the uninitiated) was evidently not what they were used to, so they added a couple of noughts, assuming the fueller had forgotten!

Sadly, on the way back to Basingstoke, things went wrong again. I was useless at navigation (don't tell my students) in the early days. We got lost again! This time, 'unsure of our position' and, once again before we ran out of fuel, I decided to land in a field. The field that I chose happened to be a wheat field.

Unfortunately, during my training, never was I told, "Don't land in a wheat or corn field unless there is nowhere else to go." We, nevertheless, ignorant of this, found it out the hard way. Yes, we set up for a normal landing and yes, we flared at normal height—but the problem was, and still is, high crops like wheat act rather like an arrester hook on an aircraft carrier which stops an aircraft very short, very quickly. The wheat wraps around the undercarriage and stops an aircraft quickly from 65 mph in about 15 feet. It pulled us up fast, causing the Shadow to hit the ground, snapping the nosewheel tube and sending the right wing forward, bending its spar. It had now just turned out to be a very expensive day!

We walked to find the farmer whose land it was and asked him where we were, before getting a taxi so that we could pick up the car and trailer to recover the aircraft. We had to get the aircraft dismantled and carted off in the trailer and not a moment too soon, as we had heard that the local press were on their way with a photographer. So, we left quickly, aircraft and all, and sure enough, when we were on our way home, I received a call from the local reporter, asking me if flying was dangerous. Of course, I replied, and truthfully, "No!" No news was good news for us that day.

It is funny with the hundreds, possibly thousands of flights every day, if one aircraft has an incident, you are always asked the question, "Is flying safe?"

Now, for those who want to learn from my experience and over my 36 years of having had fourteen engine failures and two near-misses, two bird strikes including the buzzard swooped down to attack us going through the screen, and in later years, an electrical fire soon after take-off.

Important things to note while as a student flying microlights with high-revving single-ignition two-stroke engines.

Now, this is my advice—if you have to land in a wheat or corn field—which, I suggest that you only select such a field if there is no other option, for example, if the engine has failed   then this would be the plan to expect that the wheat will grab the undercarriage and wheels as you come in to land so my advice is to come in at a safe slow landing speed on the approach but when you flare, i.e., transitioning the descent to the field into flying level but above the field, then flare higher than normal, keeping above the wheat and let the aircraft slow down and gently stall the last three feet or so.

By this time, you will be slow with less forward speed, you might land a little hard on the wheels or even slightly splay the undercarriage, but that will be the better option, because another nuisance is that wheat fields underneath are normally not flat but with ploughed ruts, so a slow speed is better. That said, only stall into the field from the flare, that is, about three feet above the ground above the wheat.

The Open Day at HMS, Daedalus was approaching, but we were still waiting for parts, so the aircraft was still broken. Not willing to let the HMS Daedalus Commander down, I managed to fix the nose leg and temporarily repair the fuselage. I'm not sure how I did it but, leaving the wings in the open trailer when we had the visiting public looking at the fuselage, nobody seemed to notice that the Shadow was slightly broken, so our appearance at the show was a success! Well, it cost me about £8000 to replace the 'D' boxes—they are the front halves of the wings—and to rebuild the aircraft, which was a lot of work. I decided that my navigation had to improve and quick, if only for the sake of my wallet!

Navigation was really hard thirty years ago—and even harder before that. We used a combination of 'dead reckoning' and map reading. Let me explain. Being an aviator is in many ways similar to being a mariner. Say, you wanted to sail across the channel from Dover to Calais many years ago. You would draw a line on your map to represent your route, you would then use a protractor (to measure angles with respect to True North or even Magnetic North if your chart showed that), and using the Magnetic North, you would get a compass heading.

If you were an experienced captain of your ship, you would be able to estimate the water current's strength and direction and so, determine a heading to steer. Those calculations, even if approximate, would allow you to steer your ship, pointing it upstream against the current, so that you would end up at Calais or very near—if you were good and if your knowledge of water currents was correct.

This method of navigation, Dead Reckoning, though, was difficult and not reliable.

If you are flying an aircraft and crossing land, you can combine dead reckoning with map reading. When reading a map, you can add 'waypoints' to your dead-reckoning line, drawn from, say, Redhill to Birmingham. You would add these waypoints on the route: they could be anything—like reservoirs, railways, roads, towns, TV masts, bridges and coastlines—the more unique (and therefore easily identifiable) the better. For example, from Redhill to Sandown on the Isle of Wight, because you have to avoid flying through controlled airspace (unless you obtain permission), e.g., Gatwick Airport's airspace, you would have to draw lines first to the west, towards a little town called Gomshall, then change course to the southwest.

So, on taking off from Redhill, your first waypoint could be the town of Dorking, next is Gomshall where, by chance, you see that there is a caravan sales business next to the railway—so, lots of caravans can be seen from the air. Let's hope the caravan sales carry on trading as if they pack up we will lose our landmark—then you alter course southwest, and in the distance, you should see Dunsfold Aerodrome, now largely disused apart from some light industry (though there is some flying there, there is no 'Control Zone'). After Dunsfold, there is a TV mast on high ground near the town of Midhurst, a good waypoint. Past that, you see the coast and as you pass over that, still on your line, there are two forts in the Solent, good landmarks they are as you see the island in front of you and, looking at your map, Sandown is to the South of the Island on the eastern side. Voila!

Finally, I would point out that you need to work out the time between waypoints and the time at which you should reach each one, from the distance to the next waypoint. Keeping to your times and getting to each waypoint confirms that your heading and timing is correct.

Navigation was still difficult, though, especially if the weatherman got the wind strength or direction, or both, wrong: and, if on the day, you compounded that error by not sticking to your plan, not flying at the planned speed, or by deviating from your planned course. You could then be in deep trouble. I always told my students to fly their planned route at the correct speed, height and compass heading: then, if the next waypoint was to the left when it should have been under the aircraft, they could blame the weatherman for the error—or the possibility that the compass was misreading—but if they didn't stick to plan, it was all a mess, and they had only themselves to blame.

Dead reckoning, combined with map reading, was far from perfect but the best we had at the time.

Now, today, of course, thirty-three years on, technology—which is just like the airliners' technology—is there to help us. We have 'Global Positioning Systems' (GPS) to help us, satellites in space; and cheap, too, the magic 'Apple iPad' or other 'tablets' with applications which, when installed, draw a magenta line for us to follow from A to B. If the line were to take us through Gatwick's Airspace, we could simply put a finger on it and move the line elsewhere to avoid that airspace—and that's it. Marvellous!

Prior to take-off, we press the 'go flying' button and a little aircraft appears on screen. That's your aircraft and as you fly, the aircraft moves, and you steer the aircraft to follow the line. 'Skydemon' and other GPS systems are a Godsend. Anthony and I would not, in later years, have flown from Redhill to Majorca without it (see end chapter for full story). Well, we could have done the eight-and-a-half-hour flight with the combination of dead reckoning and map reading, but gosh, it would have been so difficult, tiring and stressful.

In the early days before I became a flying instructor and didn't have a flying school (and of course, when I was much younger and better-looking), I was a student pilot, not very experienced at dealing with engine failures: and I remember my hero, Brian Cosgrove, who then ran the British Microlight Aircraft Association, who gave me a few words of advice. Brian was such a nice, proactive man who did a lot for the British Microlight Aircraft Association and microlight aircraft and, more importantly, always helped the members—as you would expect from the leader of an association of like-minded people.

I read that Brian had started as a meteorologist and flew an early microlight aircraft himself, so he was also 'one of us' (we flyers, that is). His legacy is his book, 'The Microlight Flying Handbook', which I still recommend to my students on their pilot's licence route today.

I was a young, inexperienced pilot, and apart from speaking to Brian on the telephone, I had only met him in person a couple of times. One such time was at Popham airfield when I had just got my pilot's licence.

He said to me, and I quote, "Have you had an engine failure yet?"

I replied, "No, Brian." (Forgetting the engine trouble my instructor Brian in Yorkshire had had with my new Shadow.)

He replied, "Get ready."

Those words stuck with me, for at that time, we were flying an aircraft with a little, underpowered, two-cylinder, two-stroke engine that had only one ignition system, and unfortunately, seventy per cent of engine failures were due to ignition failures. Now, technology has moved us on. We now fly with dual-ignition, four-stroke engines—much safer—with two separate ignition systems: these engines are able to lose one ignition system and stay running.

That said, at the time of which I speak, we were still not into such technology and, further to Brian's warning, with those little two-stroke engines during my flying career, I have suffered more than fourteen engine failures—full stoppage or partial power failures, particularly in my early career. Each one was part of a learning curve, for that little two-stroke was high-revving and, because of the importance of aircraft weight restrictions, lightweight, underpowered and overworked.

On one particular day, I was flying circuits at Redhill Aerodrome. Everything was going well until on one circuit, I started downwind, and I heard the little two-stroke engine lose all power. Now, luckily, the Shadow, like most microlights, had really good glide characteristics. In other words, it took time to come down, so the pilot could normally get the aircraft to a field—but, of course, there was no time to dwell on what had just happened; one had to have a plan; no time to freeze.

I was lucky this time, though, because I had an airfield on my right-hand side, with a runway that I had just been landing on. I called up Redhill Air Traffic Control and told them that my engine had lost all power, and I adjusted my circuit by cutting the corner between the 'downwind' leg and the 'base' leg of the circuit—as I watched the height gently decay: but the thing I did wrong (a low hours pilot, me, then) happened once I had turned onto 'finals' for the runway.

I had to fly over the M23 motorway—in itself, not a problem—and I got past the motorway but then foolishly put the flaps down as though I were flying a normal circuit with engine power. Unfortunately, the drag from the landing flap without thrust from the engine was now destroying my lovely glide! I realised that while I was approaching the boundary of the airfield, I was falling well short of the runway.

Now, in all of us, in these circumstances, there is a very strong urge to pull back on the control column to try to 'stretch' the glide: but if you do that, the airspeed quickly decays to a dangerous figure. A sufficient loss of flying speed will stall the wings, and the aircraft will fall from the sky. I was wise to that but realised that to keep my landing speed, I would have to forget the runway numbers and instead of landing 'on the numbers', land on the lead-in to it (in the 'undershoot') albeit with the correct landing speed.

However, my problem then was that between the undershoot to the runway and the runway start, there was a hard surface taxiway running across my path—and I couldn't remember whether this taxiway was higher, lower or at the same level as the runway because, like it or not, I had now touched down and I was rapidly heading for this road to cross it at ninety degrees before running on to the actual runway. I had resigned myself to the fact that I might have to take out the nosewheel assembly had the road been higher or lower but luckily, all was level so there was no damage to my Shadow. My mistake! From experience, next time, don't put landing flaps down until you are sure that you can make the runway numbers. I tell my students that if they have made a mistake and are falling short, they can always retract the flap which will reduce drag and that should help them get to their target.

My Road to Become an Instructor.

While I was finishing my pilot's licence training at Popham and had a few hours under my belt, I saw a notice on the clubhouse notice board which read, and I quote, "Would you like to be one of the Gods?" What was this all about? And then the penny dropped. The gods they were referring to were flying instructors.

A bit arrogant, I thought, but it wasn't the notice that prompted me to become an instructor, but the fact I had now done about one hundred-and-twenty hours of personal flying and I now thought what to do next.

I worked out that while I worked for British Airways, I could spare my weekends when off to hack through the Instructors Course, and in fact completed my training as a pilot trainer in around three or four weeks, then booking up the instructor examiner sometime later.

I was also lucky that at that time, you could get a career development loan through the government and borrowed fifteen hundred pounds—well, it was in 1987 or abouts, and the advantage, was it was a very low interest rate, and better still, you didn't start payments for six months after the course had finished. Brilliant!

The problem I had now was, I was an assistant flying instructor; all I needed now was someone to work for, i.e., a qualified flight instructor, and that would prove a little difficult as Redhill did not have any microlight schools at that time.

The manager, Ken, suggested that I could start my own school at Redhill and to speak to one of their ATC guys who, by chance, also had an instructor rating, and voila! I was away.

Chapter Nine
Horizons: Becoming an Instructor

Now, the training to become an instructor is demanding. First, one has to learn how to teach, and a significant part of the first few sessions of the course is dedicated to that. And instructing is not just about climbing into an aircraft with a student and showing that student how to fly the aircraft—but later on, there is also a substantial number of 'technical knowledge' subjects (also known as 'TK' or 'ground' subjects) that an instructor must not only learn but also teach. There are too many to go into in detail here but, in general, they apply to microlight flying to a greater or lesser degree.

The areas covered include "Aviation Law"—a favourite to start with because you can't just fly anywhere at any altitude or in any conditions. Certain rules apply. Then there are "Operational Procedures", a topic which covers a multitude of subjects from getting an aircraft from its parking place or hangar and taxiing round an airfield to launching into flight at the correct weight and in balance; and what happens after you have landed.

I mentioned 'conditions'. This is a reference to whether we are to fly in daylight or at night, for example (though microlight aircraft in general are not permitted to fly at night, or in Instrument Meteorological Conditions (IMC) within United Kingdom airspace). More particularly, one has to be cognizant of the kind of weather, which might be encountered anywhere along the planned flight path, and especially weather which might prevent flight or force a flight to be terminated. So, the subject of 'Meteorology' has to be studied quite deeply.

We also have to know where we are going! I don't just mean where the destination is, but the route we plan to take and whether or not controlled airspace needs to be avoided or crossed, and whether and when permission to cross is required. This is where 'navigation' comes in—estimating journey times given the prevailing winds, calculating 'waypoints', finding and marking them on an aeronautical navigation chart, planning diversions 'just in case of'; and noting those areas of controlled airspace likely to be encountered en route. Setting up the planned route on an electronic navigation device if you use one (and the CAA recommends that you do, as a backup to your plan) is also important—and requires training in itself.

Now, it's not mandatory in the United Kingdom (outside controlled airspace) to communicate with anyone while you are flying. However, most aerodromes will have at least an 'air-ground' radio service—and so do some 'farm strips'— so it is wise to have an understanding of 'aeronautical communications', the special terminology used; and the procedures used at aerodromes by air traffic controllers. So, a licence to operate an aeronautical radio station in an aircraft is a requirement for anyone operating at an airfield where there is an Aeronautical Information Service or Air Traffic Control—and 'radiotelephony' is, therefore, another subject to be mastered.

Of course, no one should fly if they are feeling 'under the weather', in particular when he or she might feel unwell, or perhaps be angry or disturbed by something, or be on medication which might impair judgement or the ability to handle machinery. Nor should anyone fly when feeling under stress or fatigued: and certainly, no one should fly when under the influence of alcohol. All this is described in another TK subject known as 'Human Performance and Limitations'.

Now, we come to the aircraft itself. Knowledge of the aircraft that one is to fly is self-evidently important, and there is no substitute for familiarity with it: but so is knowledge about the aircraft in general, and that is covered, too. Last but not the least, we have a subject called 'Flight Performance and Planning'.

This is about how the aircraft behaves when it is fully loaded, partially loaded, fully fuelled or partially fuelled (i.e., prepared for a flight) and what is required for a particular planned flight—and so on. One must have sufficient fuel for the planned flight and an appropriate diversion planned (I emphasise planning deliberately) in case of problems that necessitate adjustment of the route or a change of destination; even a return to the point of departure might be necessary on some occasions.

So, you see, that there is much more to becoming an instructor than might appear at first sight!

During my instructor training, my teacher would teach me how to teach a part of the training syllabus, say, "Teach me Exercise 8 Performance Climbing and Descending." Then, we would go and fly the exercise and then we would swap roles, and it would be my turn to teach him and so on until we had covered all the parts of the syllabus.

Once we had finished the course, another examiner would be called in to fly with me, and of course, he would ask me to teach him part of the syllabus and throw in extras like a simulated engine failure, a stall recovery and a landing, and then if, that was not enough, I would be tested on the ground subjects, Human Performance, Air Law, Aeroplanes, Navigation and Meteorology, and of course, as an instructor, sadly, that test comes around every three years (previously every two years).

After eighteen tests in my flying career, I am much better than in my early days.

I did, nevertheless, try to simplify things and develop my own terminology, like a small amount would be laughed at when I told the student move the stick just a 'gnats cock' because everyone knew that a gnats cock is very small. Gary used to laugh at that.

Chapter Ten
Our Club in the Southeast Corner

Having qualified as an instructor, I decided that I also needed to start my own flying club. This was for safety as well as social reasons as having other club members to confer with is definitely an advantage to make you a safer pilot, for example, I tell my students about all the things I did wrong so that they can learn from my mistakes and hopefully do something different—remember the wheat field.

I was able to set one up at Redhill Aerodrome, in Surrey. The experience though, was not without pitfalls, and excitement.

Our club was based in one corner of the aerodrome at Redhill, well out of the way of the main flying area. We had a good club atmosphere, with our little portacabin where we had our office and rest area. The portacabin was a large one, and it was home for our club. We had also obtained some surplus paving slabs from the local council and laid some walkways with hard areas. It was a good site for a club.

On many occasions, we would have an Open Day barbecue with the whole club involved. The idea was to introduce the public to the sport of flying.

I took on a business partner, Clive, who shared the cost of buying a new aircraft and selling said aircraft into shares. The business plan was such that you learnt to fly on the Shadow, and after you got your Pilot Licence, you could buy a share of the aircraft. It was a good plan when the aircraft cost £18000; not good now—the aircraft cost £140,000.

Anyway, one Open Day, I had invited my business partner's wife, Emma, to come for a flight in the afternoon, in the Shadow—and she accepted. We had a very busy Open Day with lots of people attending.

I put Emma in the front seat of the Shadow—the best seat in the house. It was like being in a glider with the canopy shut. You had no engine to block your vision, as the engine was behind with a 'pusher' propellor; and the person in the front was sitting ahead of the wings, so there was nothing to impair that fantastic view.

With Emma strapped into the front of the Shadow, I closed the canopy over her and got myself into the back seat. We taxied out to the holding point (commonly called 'the hold'). The Open Day at the club was in full swing, with business partner Clive acting as host, talking with the potential customers who were there.

I lined up the Shadow on Runway 26 Left (26L) and opened the throttle. The aircraft accelerated along the grass runway and, with Emma being very light, the aircraft leapt off the runway and into the air. We climbed away, and during the climb, I asked the control tower if I might do a non-standard left turn instead of the standard normal right turn so that I could fly right over the clubhouse Open Day. With permission granted—and once I had got to my desired height and we were above the clubhouse—I pulled back on the throttle and lifted the nose, flying the Shadow so slowly that, with the wind against me, the Shadow looked as though it was almost at a standstill. That was impressive and I knew that it was.

I held the aircraft in that position for a few seconds, then lowered the nose, powered up and flew off eastwards. I could see all eyes were on us from the people on the ground. Emma loved it and was ecstatic about her experience. What I couldn't see, but found out from friends later, was that as I flew over Emma's husband, Clive (my business partner). His mouth was wide open and remained open until I powered the Shadow up again to fly away to the east.

Shadow was a remarkable, safe little aircraft. It was very safe with no defined stall. (A stall occurs when there is insufficient lift from the wings to maintain flight). It was a fantastic glider, handy if you had problems with that little two-stroke engine in flight! It was easy to fly, and it was easy to land. The Shadow, though, had poor ground-handling characteristics. It was very light and therefore very susceptible to damage from wind when on the ground. The wings were long and very light and if the wind got under a wing it could easily turn the aircraft over.

One morning, everyone was flying, but at about midday, the weather suddenly changed, and a strong wind warning came from the Met office—winds were going to be gusting from almost nothing in the morning to forty knots. I was off that day, when one of our students, a doctor, was flying a solo cross-country flight and had reached his destination, Goodwood Aerodrome (near Chichester, West Sussex) before the wind increased.

My other instructor, Jim, phoned Goodwood Airfield where the Air Traffic Service at our request told the doctor not to risk flying back, but instead, to put the aircraft safely in a hangar: and Jim would drive to Goodwood to collect him. Most of the other Shadows flying in the local area had landed and were back at the Redhill base, tied down safely. There was just one Shadow left that had gone to Headcorn Airfield, in Kent. We were not worried about that one because the pilot was low-qualified, though he had some hours under his belt. We therefore assumed that he would not risk flying back to Redhill, but instead, would put the Shadow in a hangar there and call us for a pickup. How wrong we were! Instead, even though the pilot, Steven, knew about the sudden increasing wind, he nevertheless decided to attempt to fly back to Redhill.

Now, adding to what I have already said, the Shadow could fly in nearly any weather without no concerns—but what was risky was landing and getting the aircraft back to our club without it turning over after landing, especially in a forty-knot wind. With lesser winds, it was not unusual to have two people—one on each wingtip—holding the aircraft while taxiing, so that the wind could not get under a wing and turn the aircraft over. Well, to our surprise, the guys saw Steven approaching to land, almost stationary in the sky because of such a strong wind blowing against him. He landed OK but stupidly exited the runway before the lads could get to him to grab the Shadow's wingtips. So now, he had the force of 40 knots on one wingtip.

With the engine still running and him still sat in the cockpit, the wind lifted the aircraft back into the air and flipped it straight over. The wings were flat on the ground, the wheels were poking in the air, propellor still spinning; and the engine was running at idle, with fuel from the fuel tank seeping into the ground! Steven was OK, though. He shut down the aircraft and clambered out—but now, the aircraft needed over nine thousand pounds worth of repair work to be done to it! Almost as bad, when I asked why he had (foolishly) flown back from Headcorn in those horrendous winds, I was not impressed by his answer, which was—and I quote: "How would I have got back home?"

There is a well-known saying which instructors tell their students, for a particular attitude of mind has killed many pilots. We call it "Get-you-home-itis". This is the compulsion to fly the aircraft in any weather because you need to get home or need to be somewhere. Of course, the correct course of action is to hangar or tie down the aircraft and take the train or the bus or even a commercial flight instead. Anyway, my day off that day with Steven destroying the Shadow was ruined.

I have always driven an old car, I suppose, because I am lucky. As an aircraft engineer, I can repair them myself—saving lots of money—so it has benefitted my wallet. At one time, I had a lovely old blue Mercedes 'E Class'. It was a lovely big car, with a six-cylinder, three-litre engine, fast and comfortable, and surprisingly for its size, it was good on fuel. My Mercedes had a very big boot, and as the aircraft use the same fuel as that which we put in our cars—motor gasoline ('Mogas') it was a regular task for me to load the boot of the car with four fuel cans, yellow ones and red ones, for a trip to the local garage to get fuel for our aircraft.

When you have many students and pilots from all walks of life from plumbers to bankers to office workers and most with no mechanical knowledge, you have to try to make fuelling the aircraft easy and as foolproof for them as you can.

The problem we had was that all our Shadow aircraft had two-stroke engines. The two-stroke does not have lubricating oil in the sump of the engine; in fact, it has no sump at all, so the only way you can provide lubrication to the engine is by adding two-stroke oil to the fuel before it goes into the engine to be ignited. That lubricates the working parts of the engine: the fuel provides power, and the oil lubricates the moving parts at the same time.

We had three Shadow aircrafts for which you had to premix the fuel and oil (add oil to the can of fuel) with the fuel and oil in correct proportions: too much would generate poor performance with a smoky exhaust, and too little would be worse, with the engine starved of lubricating oil, overheating, and quickly seizing solid as the surface friction between moving parts of the unlubricated engine ruined it. We would premix the oil with the petrol in the red cans.

Now two of our aircraft were slightly different. These had a metering valve system with a separate oil tank for two-stroke oil that would feed an injector pump. As you opened up the throttle to speed up the engine, more oil would be fed to the engine than was fed to the engine at idle power. The advantage to these aircrafts was better oil fuel mixing, whether at idle (less oil) or at full power when it required more oil. The aircraft that had the metering pump and their own oil tanks used unmixed motor fuel straight from the garage pump, and that fuel we put into the yellow fuel cans; in other words, in the yellow cans was pure gasoline with no oil added.

We didn't stop there with trying to make things idiot-proof. We also had two small pumping fuel bowsers and, you may have guessed it, one was yellow that was for neat petrol, with no oil therein, and a red bowser which contained fuel and oil, mixed by us from the red fuel cans. 'Murphy proof', eh? Well, if only!

The Shadow had only enough fuel for one-and-three-quarter-hours flying with a doubtful fifteen minute reserve, so we encouraged each pilot after each flight to refill the aircraft fuel tank ready for his cohort. This always gave the next pilot a safe full fuel tank. Yet, we still occasionally spotted a pilot filling the aircraft from the wrong-coloured bowser. It was normally the same pilot, not mechanically minded, one who was always too busy and just wanted to fly, then get on with his busy day.

For example, years before, I did have a student who worked in the city. He used to open the throttle and increase the speed of the aircraft on the tail end of the lesson, and when I asked what the rush was to get back, he would tell me he had an appointment to play golf. Of course, with always in a rush, flying was dangerous not for him; luckily, he lost interest and didn't get his pilot's licence. I say that kindly in that this was the type of person who would be very likely to have an accident or cause one once a pilot, as they are always in a rush.

I remember, when I was being taught by Brendon in Yorkshire, a gentleman came to find out about flying talking to Brendon.

After the man had left, I said to Brendon, "New student, Brendon?"

"No," he replied, "he has come into some money and can't decide whether to buy a sports car, a boat, or an aeroplane, so I suggested a boat."

"That's not good for business, Brendon," I replied.

"Look, Phil, you need a bit more commitment to be a safe pilot."

I then understood where he was coming from.

One day, one of our best Shadows took off, and while it was flying over Kent, the engine stopped abruptly. The pilot 'froze' for 50 seconds, and while the aircraft was gliding down, the pilot burnt up all his valuable time, frozen, doing nothing; and in so doing, failed to find a good field for a landing and so, hit a tree. The aircraft hit the ground hard (the pilot was just a passenger), right wing first, so hard that the wing disintegrated—but the collapse of the wing absorbed all the energy and the pilot, thankfully, hobbled away—but had broken a leg and an arm.

The Shadow was made of a honeycomb material called 'Fibrelam', amazing stuff, about half an inch thick, with a honeycomb core. It is the same stuff that airliner floorboards and Formula One cars are made of. The good thing about Fibrelam was, though very expensive, it was strong, absorbed energy and vibration, protecting the pilot. We have all seen those terrible crashes of the racing drivers where the car somersaults and scrapes along the ground yet to everyone's relief, the driver walks away with only cuts and bruises. Well, the Shadow was like that Formula One racing car. The aircraft designer was a bit like a Barnes Wallace (he of 'bouncing bomb' fame) of microlight design—a brilliant man.

After the engine failure over Kent, I stripped down the engine from the crashed Shadow which, of course, was a write-off. I found that the crankshaft bearings had seized because of no oil lubrication. Evidently, our red-can-yellow-can system had failed. Still not 'Murphy proof', as we always used to say in engineering. There will always be someone trying to force a square peg into a round hole. The sad thing was that the previous pilot after enjoying his flight had, through his desire to get away and thus carelessness, caused this bad accident to his fellow pilot on the next flight.

Our Saboteur

With regard to my fuel uplift trips to the local garage and petrol and oil mixing, on one particular day, I loaded up the Mercedes with the fuel containers and headed off to pick up fuel from the garage. I filled one container, and when it was full, I started filling another one. Then, somebody shouted from another pump, "Fuel on the forecourt!" And to my astonishment, I saw that fuel was running from the boot of my blue Mercedes onto the forecourt surface. I quickly lifted the leaking can and syphoned out the fuel into another empty can. While doing this, I saw that the leaking can had been deliberately punctured through the side a number of times. The holes in the can were square and, I suspected, maliciously made by my own square welder's metal chipping hammer: and, after having driven back to the airfield, Arthur and I found more sabotaged, empty, fuel cans in our fuel store, all punctured by the same tool, a tool which belonged to us. A saboteur was amongst us.

It was extremely unpleasant, driving a potential bomb back from the garage with a swimming pool of fuel in the boot and with the overwhelming smell of petrol. Having all the windows open helped a bit—but not much. It took many weeks for the smell of petrol to leave the car. As I have said many times, aviation, sadly, attracts some strange and undesirable people, who are often quietly amongst us acting as normal friends of the club. We never found the culprit, so instead, had to increase security. We put up CCTV cameras, and most importantly, checked the fuel cans before we filled them!

We were getting busier, and apart from my very first CFM Shadow G-MTMY, my partner Clive and I decided that we needed another aircraft. We went Essex-way to view another Shadow which was for sale, a G-MWEZ that was stored in a specially made 'Tee' box-type hangar, one that just covered the wings, tail and fuselage, with little room for anything or anyone else. The condition of the aircraft was hard to judge as it had evidently not moved for a long while, judging by the layer of dust covering it. We took a chance and started to negotiate a price. Clive, being a Mason, as was the owner, struck a deal, and we now owned another aircraft to add to the school. To our pleasant surprise, when we washed the Shadow, underneath that dirt, there was a lovely little aircraft, better than we had expected. We now had two aircraft in our fleet, while we were also building a 'Shadow' from a kit in Clive's garage.

A Tee Hangar is one which mimics the shape of the aircraft. If you were to fly over it, the wings would be enclosed in the top end of the tee with the fuselage in the long part. It was a cheaper way of keeping your aircraft protected from the weather. This one had a number of doors that dropped to allow the wings to come out.

When we trailered the aircraft back home and started to wash it, all that dust and dirt came off, and there was a very good aircraft under that dirt. We didn't buy the Tee Hangar, though, so we were now with two aircrafts in need of hangarage.

We were over at the east side of the airfield, and it was a friendly part of the airfield. I think that this was not by accident: microlight flying was new, and I think that Redhill management thought it better to separate this small new business with strange-looking aeroplanes from the mainstream and apparently up-market big boys. Anyway, lots of people commented how friendly our side of the field was compared to the other side, and our club membership grew bigger and bigger.

There was a small work area next to the open hangar that was originally a cowshed. It had a door and was about the size of a very large garage, but as we could quickly remove the wings from the Shadows (we couldn't get them in otherwise), it suited our needs at this time. It had originally had one glider inside, the owner having a trolley to put the aircraft in sideways, one wing first then the other. When he left, it was not much good for anyone except for us, as it was not practical for other aircraft owners whose aircraft had non-removal wings.

We, by then, had built G-MZBN from a kit (an aircraft of which bad-tempered Tim—more of whom later—had been a part owner) the aircraft going from a heap of parts to an actual flying machine—and we were now able to house all these aircraft wings in our little garage hangar, especially if bad weather was forecast. We had electricity, too, sub-metered from our friends across the road—a maintenance facility for the only other flying school on the airfield during this time.

Now, we needed another office and recreational area, and for that, luckily, we were not far from the village of Rusper where there was a company that sold second-hand portacabins of different sizes, some in various stages of redecoration and cheap enough for a little business like ours to buy. We bought a two-room porta cabin, quite big, comfortable and suitable for our needs. We were now set up with our aircraft, three of them hangered: and we had a cosy office and recreational lounge which doubled as a briefing room and somewhere where we could do night school on the five aircraft subjects: Air Law, Meteorology, Human Performance, Navigation and Aircraft Technical.

The early morning call that you really don't want to receive is one announcing the destruction of your aircraft. It had been a really stormy night, winds had unexpectedly got up beyond forty knots and our best wide-body Shadow was out in this weather, albeit tied down. Unfortunately, Redhill has soil with high clay content, and along with the wind, it rained hard so with the wings rocking back and forward in the wind and the rain making the ground go mushy, the tie-downs lost their grip and, at some time during the night, the aircraft broke free. The wind then got under the wing, and the aircraft went flying on its own before re-landing upside down, severely broken and impaled against another aircraft.

So, at about nine-thirty the next morning, I received a call from Redhill ATC, asking me to retrieve my broken aircraft.

I stumbled across a video on YouTube that was of a lovely-looking aircraft on an airfield (not ours, I hasten to add) on the hard standing outside a hangar, not tied down, and the CCTV camera on the hangar recorded the aircraft being written off by the wind. First, the nose of the aircraft went up and then went back down on to the ground; then, another gust came and up the nose went again—and this time, a stronger gust came along, and this one lifted the nose and then the wings. The aircraft was now hovering as though it were a helicopter in the hover; but then, a stronger wind lifted the nose further while the aircraft was hovering, and the aircraft went vertical before it rotated backwards, going upside down and flying inverted out of view of the camera with the aircraft's shadow following. The aircraft went out of camera shot, but you can guess that it had blown about thirty feet, landed upside down and destroyed itself.

I know how the owner pilot must have felt when he got the news. I didn't see my aircraft go over as that had happened in the middle of the night—and that was probably just as well, as a video of that might not have made me feel any better!

On another occasion, serious damage was caused by vandalism. It was a lovely morning, but when I got to the east gate and drove through, I looked over towards our club, and I had to do a 'double take'. I noticed a 'Cessna 152' belonging to another flying school that looked very peculiar. The tail was broken! Christ! I was trying to analyse in my head what sort of heavy landing the pilot had done that would cause such damage. The aircraft, too, I knew, was the chief flying instructor's favourite aircraft! At this time, I was coming to the end of the dirt road, and, to my horror, I saw one of our own pilots' Flight Design 'CT' aircraft moved from its normal tie-down position and in a very sorry state.

The aircraft had been tied down with the tie-downs tied to the aileron and flap horns, but now, it looked as though a tornado had ripped the flaps off, leaving the tie-downs still attached to the ground. Our 'Jabiru' aircraft then caught my eye: this was down on its nose; the nose leg was broken, and the tail was pointing skywards. The Jabiru didn't *look* too badly damaged—but it was.

Then I noticed the 'Rans' aircraft owned by our club member, Ken, impaled sideways against the other flying school's twin-engine 'Seneca' aircraft. Then, I saw the fire service, accompanied by the aerodrome manager—and realised that what I was looking at was sabotage. But what about the four school Shadows on the tree line, all tied down? I rushed over to them with a nervous lump in my throat. They were all untouched. Whether the darkness had hidden them next to the line of trees, I am not sure, but at least that meant that our flying school was still able to operate.

The truth of the story was beginning to unfold when the police arrived with forensics. An old commercial pilot, Max, had parked his old Ford Granada—a big car—in the club's car park, untaxed, abandoned and not started for quite some time. On this particular night, in the very early hours, two or three vandals had cut the lock on the east gate, broken into Maxwell's Ford Granada and, even after all the time that the car had been laid up there, managed to start the car.

After that, these vandals started pummelling the aircraft with the Granada, driving into them again and again. It was a disaster area with thousands and thousands of pounds worth of damage. Later that day, the insurance assessors were nervously on scene, for they were trying to work out which company insured which aircraft, hoping that it wouldn't be just one insurance company so that the expected claims would be shared.

Sadly, while the destruction made headline news, the culprits were never caught—though the forensic team found drugs in the Ford Granada.

Alex's CT was a write-off; so was our Jabiru aircraft. Ken's Rans was written off, as was the Cessna 152 belonging to the other flying school. Fortunately, our Cessna 150 Aerobat was still in Spain—see later—otherwise, I am sure that that aircraft would have been pummelled, too. What the motive was for breaking into the airfield, deliberately destroying aircraft and causing upset to all of us, we will never know. The world is full of very strange people.

After saying that, a particularly strange person does come to mind: whether he was responsible for this, we will never know—I suppose it could have been anyone.

This person started learning to fly with me. He was a young guy, in his twenties; and he was progressing well. He was a bit snappy with the other club members, but we ignored that. He became sufficiently proficient to fly solo, and he did that, his first solo flight, in the newest school aircraft and that finished his circuit training. He was in a hurry to progress and wanted to do some more solo flying so, this time, I let him use the new aircraft again—which was OK.

He asked me if I knew of a bed and breakfast place where he could stay when he was flying. I recommended one that I knew of in Horley, run by a nice Irish couple, where I had stayed once. It was nice; they were good people, easy to get on with; and I even offered to have a word with them and book him in if he wanted me to—which he did.

After he'd stayed there for two days, I asked the lad how he was getting on in his new 'digs', but the response that I got was not what I expected! He did nothing but moan about everything: I was very surprised. It didn't add up. I then received a telephone call from the young Irish lady, saying that they had asked him to leave because he was rowing with them and complaining about nearly everything. Well, you can understand how bad I felt being the one who booked him in and the one who told them he was 'OK'. Anyway, after that, I let him find his own alternative accommodation.

He came in one day to fly solo again, and I gave him G-BN to fly, but he was not happy with that. He wanted the newest wide-body Shadow. "No," I said, "I need that for training a student." He threw his toys out of the pram, insisting that he fly the aircraft that he wanted. The aircraft flew in exactly the same way, but the new aircraft was slightly bigger—so, I stuck to my guns and told him G-BN or nothing. Nothing, he accepted—as he swore at me and left the club. That was after I had signed his logbook, bringing it up to date. I never saw the young lad again.

Some months later, I had a call from the chief flying instructor of another school, located about one hundred and fifty miles away. He wanted to know about this lad, and I asked him, "Why?" It appears the lad had joined this new school. There was no problem with that, in itself. However, it also appeared that he had had a few lessons and again flown solo and then had gone to the pub with a couple of other club members and, during the conversation with the others, he had caused concern by saying that his reason for wanting to become a pilot was to smuggle drugs!

The club members had been so concerned by what they had heard that they reported it to the chief flying instructor, and after that, the CFI did not want to continue this student's training. The CFI had taken the trouble to call me to hear my story, and I bought him up to speed. It also seems the CFI had contacted the CAA for advice but later called me again and said the CAA had been sympathetic to the student! The CFI told me that nevertheless, he was still not going to teach him as he felt there was something peculiar. I think he was right and feel it was a close escape for all of us.

Our club, by now based in our large porta cabin with an office and a lounge area, needed more hangar space as our fleet of Shadows grew. In fact, we now had five Shadows, a replaced Jabiru, which we had built, and a Cessna 150 'Aerobat' with which we could also offer Single-Engine Piston (Land) (commonly called SEP(L)) training. Our Cessna, by chance, had the same registration as our website—that was, 'The Flying School', for its registration was G-BTFS. Unfortunately, while the seller seemed genuine with a perfect maintenance logbook detailing maintenance on the aircraft, I did catch a cold when we bought it. The aircraft had had a brand-new propellor fitted. Later, though, we noticed that the aircraft displayed a strange, slight vibration; not bad, but it was there all the time as though the propellor was out of balance. Surmising that that was the case, that was, of course, the first thing that I sent away to have checked and balanced. Sadly, after the propellor had been balanced, we found that the vibration was still there.

We flew the aircraft to the Costa Blanca to be used in Spain—and thereby hangs a tale in itself (see Chapter 12). While it was there, I asked the maintenance organisation to 'troubleshoot' the niggling vibration, and when it had done that, I was told that the cylinder compressions were lower than they ought to have been and the maintenance organisation recommended four new cylinders, new cylinders were fitted. When the aircraft was flying again, I asked my man, James, in Spain, "How was the vibration?"

'Better' was the reply—not quite the answer I really wanted!

When the aircraft came back to Redhill Aerodrome, I spoke to my maintenance organisation in the UK about the historic vibration. They suggested first the propellor, but that was already done; next, that the carburettor be looked at. Well, as an experienced licenced engineer myself, and having had all the cylinders changed, I thought that the problem must be more than just a carburettor fault. In fact, I suspected the bottom end of the 'Continental' engine—specifically, the crankshaft: and that turned out to be exactly where the fault was.

We removed the engine and sent it to an engine-building specialist. The specialist confirmed my diagnosis and told me that the reason for the vibration was that the crankshaft was bent and tended to seize in its bearings. I can now only assume that the aircraft, before I bought it, had had a 'propellor-strike' (i.e., the propeller had hit the ground at some stage, putting the engine under sudden severe shock) and what should have been done before the new propellor was fitted—namely, the legal requirement to strip down the engine and check the crankshaft for cracks and defects, such as being bent, and which would is always a costly exercise, evidently this—was not done, but passed on to me, sadly.

Once we got the engine back, rebuilt from the specialist, we installed it back into our Cessna, and our problems were no more.

We were still looking for more hangarage, but none was available on the airfield, so we decided to erect our own. The manager had told us that we could have anything, provided that it was classed as a temporary structure. That would be satisfactory for council planning purposes.

We employed a scaffolding firm to build a shelter hangar. It had no floor, and there was a large gap blocked with rain netting at roof height, the purpose of this being to allow the wind to pass through the top of the hangar without blowing it down. This hangar had two large barn-type metal doors, and we could get all of our aircraft about 5 then under its roof.

Unfortunately, there is always a busybody who seems to have nothing better to do than keep watch through binoculars for anything new going on at the airfield, nosily watching, ready to complain about what others are doing, and true to form, before the last clamp had been tightened on the temporary hangar, a man from the council arrived to tell us that we needed planning permission for this temporary hangar.

We managed to keep our hangar for six years until our legal fight to keep it was lost and we had to remove it. Just for good measure, the nice Council Planning Department decided to add our nice little porta cabin to the enforcement notice, which now meant that not only were we to lose our hangar, but also our clubhouse.

One of the things that I was amazed by, though, was that while the council was pushing us to get rid of our hangar, it still happily charged us thirty pounds per square foot in business rates on it—and we paid that figure until we won our appeal to reduce it to ten pounds per square foot! After all, there was a grass floor and a draughty big gap where the wall met the roof, yet the council had rated the hangar as though it had been all enclosed and centrally heated like the helicopter hangars on the other side of the airfield! Unbelievable! But even more amazing, when after the enforcement, the hangar was long gone we, of course, stopped paying business rates: after all, the hangar and porta cabin were no more. The council then threatened us with legal action for arrears of business rates—until I asked them if they talked to one another across the room, explaining that the hangar was no more and so, that business rates were also no more. It's frightening really, how stupid these 'people in charge' can really be.

Were pleased, though, that we enjoyed our hangar and porta cabin for six years while fighting the enforcement notice in the courts with the help of our solicitor—though we did, on occasion, have some flooding issues. Close to us was a fast-flowing stream, and there were many winters when the water didn't soak into the clay soil or run off through the nearby stream, but instead, the stream overflowed, and a tidal wave flooded our hangar and the immediate area. Luckily, our porta cabin stood above the ground on legs, so that was OK, but I remember opening our hangar to find our two railway sleepers floating around the aircraft like crocodiles and our twenty-two-foot trailer floated like a boat, blown against the hangar, luckily jamming itself, complete with Shadow aircraft, inside.

Inside the hangar, all the other aircraft looked very peculiar with their wheels submerged, and two days later, after the water had gone, we were into removing wheels and changing all the wheel bearings. The wheels don't take kindly to living underwater!

In an effort to stop the flooding, we made a pit and installed a float-operated water pump that would switch on automatically and start to remove the water through ditches back to the stream—but, of course, this only worked when the stream water level was low. Once it overflowed, it was like the tide coming in rather than going out. If it overflowed, our little pump got submerged as well with nowhere to pump the water—but otherwise, it was a good idea.

Eventually, I decided to upgrade our aircraft. Remembering our students, Alex now a fully trained pilot, had bought an aircraft called a 'CT', built by a German company, 'Flight Design'. The abbreviation 'CT' is short for 'Composite Technology' (and there are several variants of that, including the 'CTSW'—Composite Technology Short Wing). The aircraft had dual controls. This was a nice, safe and fast, touring aircraft—and ideal for training with two control sticks and side-by-side seating.

I had to use my own savings, about fifty-two thousand pounds, as you could never get a bank loan as a company, which enabled me to buy one of these fantastic aircraft myself. The aircraft was fast, with a huge cockpit; and it leapt past our little Shadows in flight.

When my aircraft was available, the agent, Oscar, flew it to Redhill from Sywell aerodrome and gave me a forty-five-minute training session in it before we set off back from Redhill to Sywell, so that Oscar could get back home. Once we got to Sywell and I bade goodbye to Oscar, I was on my own, in a brand-new aircraft, twice as fast as the Shadow and just feeling my way. I needed to get to know the characteristics of this ultra-fast aircraft. Not only did I have to fly it, but there was no 'Skydemon' GPS navigation system in those days, so I also had to concentrate on navigating past Stanstead Airport and its controlled airspace. Christ! I had to give that one a wide berth on my way back to Redhill.

When I got nearly to the Thames Estuary, I realised that time was against me and that by the time I would arrive back at Redhill Aerodrome, it would have been shut and getting dark: so, with Southend Airport in sight and knowing Rochester would be next, I decided that it was best to head for Rochester Airport instead and to land there, this being the safe option. Also, I could tie down the aircraft for the night, call the girlfriend and get a lift back home as we lived close to Rochester.

The next morning, I returned, prepared the aircraft for flight and off I went, landing at Redhill 25 minutes later. From then on, I was on a bit of a 'learning' curve with my new CT, the tricky bit being that it was not so easy to land this fast slippery machine. Being newly introduced to the type, landing was difficult because the CT wanted to keep flying. The manufacturer, Flight Design, had on an early aircraft—mine included—put a strong spring inside the nose gear leg but not so good if, on landing, you let the nose wheel touch the ground at speed, the aircraft would enter a pitch oscillation.

As the aircraft flew along the runway to land, with the nose springing up and down, it was natural to think that these oscillations would soon damp down. Not so! In fact, they became worse, more violent, and I soon learnt very quickly that the only solution was to add full power, abandon the landing and take-off again—turning the landing into a take-off—and next time, to keep the nose off the ground on touchdown, holding the nose up as long as possible while the speed bled off. This information, I, of course, passed on to my students.

Later, thankfully, the manufacturer did a modification which changed the spring for a stack of hard nylon blocks which sorted out that problem, although, as I say to my students, one must land on the main wheels and keep the nose flying as long as possible until the speed decays. Nevertheless, I had a student, Jake, who was not easy to teach. He seemed a bit too laidback, a little like he was dreaming, sometimes. I encouraged him to 'switch on' and tried to get some alertness, aggression even, into him, especially when he was in critical phases of flight—namely, close to the ground, that is, when taking off and landing.

Now, I had another instructor, Julian, flying for me, and one day, I asked him to fly with Jake. Julian, a young Welsh lad, was an excellent instructor. He told me, though, that when he thought a student was ready to go it alone and go solo, he would put his hands under the cheeks of his bum for the student's last landing.

"Why do you do that?" I asked.

"Because it shows the student that he has full control," he replied.

"Oh dear, never do that," I told him. I remembered that disastrous trip with Dean in the Shadow.

It was later by chance that I sent Julian flying with Jake. I told Julian that Jake was good and nearly ready to fly solo but warned him nevertheless to watch Jake while he was landing and not to put his hands under his bum. After the flying lesson, Julian got out of the aircraft, and the first words out of his mouth were: "Bloody hell!"

"What happened?" I asked. Julian told me that Jake was doing OK, but then on the final landing, unexpectedly, as the ground came closer, Jake did nothing, making no attempt to land the CT. Julian, taken by surprise, had to save the aircraft. "That is precisely why you never put your hands under the cheeks of your bottom," I said.

When I quizzed Jake about what had happened to the last landing, as though in a dream, he replied, "I dunno!"

"You see what I mean, Julian?" I told him, "Always expect the unexpected. My hand is always hovering around the control column during take-off and landing, no matter who is flying or how qualified in the other seat."

Jake sometimes couldn't come as regularly as I think he needed to, but nevertheless, I later managed to get him to solo standard and after that, he did a couple more hours flying alone. We were busy, and we only had the one CT at this time. Jake wanted to do a quick half-hour with me and then announced that he wanted to go off to the east to do some more flying on his own. I flew with him first and he flew well during that flight, but while he was flying on his own, my next student Greg came in, and I told him we would have a cup of tea while we waited for G-JF to return. When we went outside in the sun to enjoy our tea, I, to my horror, noticed an aircraft upside down on the grass runway—not a pretty sight for me.

I said to Greg, "Please don't say that that is the CT, upside down on the runway!"

"Unfortunately, yes, looks like it," he replied. That was a bad ending to an otherwise beautiful day. Jake was uninjured, but the aircraft was not so good. Jake went home, leaving me to pick up the pieces. Luckily, I found a good repairer who had the aircraft flying within three weeks, so my business, though out of action temporarily, quickly got back online with G-JF repaired and airworthy again.

Unfortunately, while Jake flew and even went solo again, he was one of those laidback students who was very busy with his business and thought that he could fit flying in, as and when, which sadly, as I have said before, is a recipe for disaster. I was worried that with that situation, even if he were to obtain his pilot's licence, disaster would loom if he failed to keep up his perishable skills on a regular basis.

Flying needs a bit of commitment and constant practice, as one is always learning something new.

Another experience I recall going back in time is when my partner in business, Clive, and I decided that we would build our own 'Shadow' from a factory-supplied kit. Apart from me and Clive, we had Tim, another shareholder, helping us. That turned out to be a big mistake.

During this time, I still worked for British Airtours, a holiday charter airline, but still officially belonging to the main company, which was British Airways. I was a supervisor working on Airtours' fleet of Boeing 737s. Occasionally, Tim joined the team of engineers which I controlled, and I remember on one occasion, when we had a Number One engine change to do, Tim had got some special tools from the hangar store—these special tools being a kit unique to the engine-removal job.

When you borrowed special tools from the store, you were required to leave one of the brass discs unique to you and having your number thereon. If I remember, we each had five brass discs. They were the size of a two pence piece, allowing us to borrow special tools from the store.

When the engine change was complete and we were clearing up, we found that another young engineer had taken them back to the store, the tools that Tim had got from the store. Well, I guess that Tim had started to stress when he could not find the engine change kit to take back; and then his temper erupted when, after searching for the tools, he found that the young engineer had already returned them. I, of course, as the supervisor, stepped into the argument that erupted with the young engineer visibly stressed at being shouted at and upset. I took Tim aside to cool him down—he had a very short temper, being renowned for it.

To my surprise, in later years, when British Airtours dissolved and British Airways took over, although Tim's temper was like an erupting volcano, British Airways nevertheless promoted him to supervisor—so much for the psychological tests that he had gone through for that promotion. As you will have guessed, being in charge of a team of engineers stressed him even more and did not do anything for his health or temper except make it worse. In fact, once, Tim had got so upset with a storeman for not getting the spares that he needed for the aircraft as quickly as he had wanted that he tried to haul the poor storeman over the counter, grabbing him by his collar.

Because of this and an increasing number of other incidents, his temper got so out of control that the trade union got involved and told the BA management that the company would have to waive its policy of instant dismissal of an employee who retaliated and thumped firecracker Tim because, the union told British Airways' management, that now that management knew that there was a temper problem, it was their—management's—task to sort out the problematic Tim. The union threatened that strike action would follow if anyone were to be sacked in the very likely event of thumping Tim.

The company had to set up an anger-management course for Tim, and they sort of did do that; just chatting to him in the pub over a drink was only partially successful. In fact, the only time I saw Tim's volcanic temper subside was when the stress was gone, after his retirement.

Unfortunately, we at our club, now had Tim still working there—and still stressed—helping us to build the Shadow, as he had a share in the aircraft. Well, the build project was dragging on, and after building two aircraft in my lifetime, apart from helping to build five or six Concordes, with my many colleagues of course, this project was becoming tedious.

I can say from experience that the case when building your own aircraft is, the build occupies your mind even when you are sleeping, because you dream about it. I also realised that when the aircraft was under construction, it could have been a washing machine or a complicated lawnmower—it didn't matter; it was a static project; it was boring so to speak; but after its first flight, the aircraft was transformed from a heap of useless parts into a flying machine that was now no longer under build but an aircraft to be maintained.

A lot of the aircraft kit makers knew this: so, some of the American kit producers were crafty. They invited their interested customers over to fly in their demonstration aircraft, and the buyer of the kit would get the impression that after a few weekends spent working in the garage, he would be up at 3000 ft, flying his own finished aircraft. How taken in these customers were! There were a lot of unfinished projects on the market and, to compound the would-be-builder's misconception, the fuselage of the aircraft was supplied ready-built sufficiently by the factory, so that one could sit inside one's just-arrived aircraft fuselage, in one's garage, pretending to fly as the hope of finishing the kit got diminished or the wife's patience ran out—she having let you spend all your hours in the garage, or worse, a divorce on the horizon! So, building an aircraft, even from a kit, was no small feat.

Anyway, I didn't want to be one of the statistics of having an unfinished project up for sale, so I decided to ask one of the Airtours engineers, Eddy, to help us out with the project and to pay him for the day. The day started OK, with Eddy, Tim and I working on the Shadow, but problems occurred when I had to fly with a student and Tim and Eddy were left on their own.

Eddy, when I returned to work, told me that he and Tim had attempted to fit the wings to the Shadow for the very first time, but they would not fit. They needed to be 'fettled' (in short, smoothed and fitted). Eddy said that Tim's temper level got higher and higher with a hammer in his hands, struggling to fit the wing pins. Eddy told me that he realised that there was only one person who was there to absorb the wrath of Tim's anger; and because of this, he reluctantly told me, he could not help us anymore. That was a sad thing for me to hear, but I was not surprised.

Eventually, Tim's frustration ran its course, and as soon as he muttered to me that he wanted out of his share in the Shadow project, my chequebook was out as quick as light, and I paid him for his share. Frustratingly for Tim, he came to the airfield on the day of the aircraft's test flight and saw the Shadow all finished, freshly painted and flying over his head at 1200 feet. He was gutted when he asked whose Shadow it was, and I replied, "Ours!" Oh dear, sorry Tim!

Our business was doing well. Not only were we teaching people to fly, but people were buying shares in the aircraft, and there were many who later became instructors and flew with us, teaching more people. We had barbecues and open days and sat in the sun. It was like a very exciting holiday camp. Club members, not all flyers, came up, and if one of the aircraft had a puncture, there was always plenty of help available. It was a good, exciting place to be.

I had Ben, my dog, running around. Everyone liked him—he was part of the club, too. He, a border collie that was affected by noise if we got the vacuum cleaner out, was so funny. He would be barking while excitedly running around it. He would wait for us to start a Shadow. When we did, he would run around the aircraft many times, round and around at a great speed, always running in a right-hand circle, never left—a nut case, but a very intelligent dog in reality.

There was a travellers' camp not far from the airfield and on occasions, it was a nuisance and a danger and it stopped airfield operations, because the airfield was then an open area, and the travellers would come galloping in with horses and carts at great speed, entering by one of the eastern gate entrances and galloping right across the active runway, maybe doing a couple of circles while shouting abuse; and before anyone could stop them, they galloped out through another gate, escaping any legal action.

Then, one day, we were plagued with my most hated insects; wasps that we found had a nest near our outside fuel store. The wasps were preventing us briefing students and made themselves at home flying around in the porta cabin. Jim told me to pour some petrol into the hole.

"That will kill them," he said.

Well, Clever Dick me had decided in an addition to that plan, to pour some petrol into the hole and then, stupid me, yes, I decided to throw a flaming match into the hole; and, yes, whoof, the petrol killed the wasps OK, and it paid for them to be cremated, but then the flames started heading dangerously towards our fuel store. This wasn't in the plan, and I could only watch in horror as the flames licked closer and closer to the fuel cans while I scurried like a headless chicken, looking around for a fire extinguisher or bucket of water. Luckily for me, the flames died away just before the store. *What a wally*, I thought. Best not try that again!

A much funnier experience occurred, though, when a father and son came to the school. The father wanted us to teach the son to fly, which we attempted to do, but the funny side of it was that every time we asked the son a question, his father would answer before the poor lad could reply. Any question that we asked the son would immediately be answered by the father. It was like this, so funny, "David, did your turns go well?"

"Yes, he turned OK," the father would reply.

"David, have you anything you want to ask?"

"No, nothing," the father would answer. We did have a good laugh about it over a coffee in the clubhouse. Poor lad, he was just like the dummy in a ventriloquist's act.

Chapter Eleven
Boy Gets Unplanned, Very Long Air Experience Flight

It was a lovely hot summer's day, but my instructor Rob and I had only a couple of flights in the morning—in fact, we had both finished by two o'clock, so we had lunch. The problem was that there was an air experience flight scheduled for five o'clock. That meant that we would be doing nothing for three hours. Well, Rob asked me if I minded if he went home, leaving me to sit it out and wait for our air experience customer. I told Rob to go home, which he started to do, but then he changed his mind and decided that he would stay with me and do the air experience flight himself.

Just before five o'clock, a big group of people arrived. The person who had our air experience voucher was a young lad. With him were his mum and dad, his granddad and grandmother, sister, her husband and the grandkids. There were quite a few of the family who had come to see off this lad on his birthday air experience flight.

While Rob was briefing the young lad, I took the family into our porta cabin where I put the kettle on and made them tea. The porta cabin windows were open, but there was absolutely no wind: it was a very warm, humid day, a sticky day. I watched Rob seat the young lad in the front of the Shadow, strap him in, and then, after he had climbed through the roll bars into the back seat, I excused myself from the family and went out to the aircraft. I shouted, "Ignition switches on!" and I pulled the starter cord. After three pulls, the little Shadow two-stroke engine burst into life. I closed the front canopy on the lad and locked the two catches shut.

I stepped away, and as Rob taxied along the taxiway, towards the runway 26, I returned to the family, drinking their tea in the porta cabin, and we all stepped out into the open to watch Rob take off and head out towards the east. Rob had only been flying for about fifteen minutes when amazingly, while I stood next to the kettle by the open window talking to the family, I was suddenly hit by a gust of wind through the window. All that day, there had not been a breath or hint of any wind but now, in a second, it was windy!

I rushed outside and looked towards the west of the airfield, and there had suddenly appeared a towering black Cumulonimbus thundercloud, and it looked as though others were forming. *Oh, hell!* I thought, *Rob certainly will not be returning to Redhill in a hurry.*

I explained to the young lad's family that the weather had changed suddenly, with no forecast or warning. I explained to them that it was likely that Rob would probably land at an airfield further east; Headcorn, for example.

Well, time passed, and I sent the family home, telling them not to worry in that I would deliver their young son to them when I got a message from Rob, telling me where he had ended up. Rob did eventually call me. He told me that he was running away from the thunderclouds, the air was becoming unstable and that he did pick a field not far from our airfield in which to land but, he said, as he was on 'finals' to land, the air became very turbulent, so he had aborted the landing and gone around—climbing away and flying further out towards the east. He had eventually landed on the other side of Edenbridge, near Penshurst, in a farmer's field.

Rob had tied the aircraft down by the time I had found the farm, having driven there—easy to find from the air, not so easy when you have the car! When I arrived, Rob and the young lad were drinking tea supplied by the friendly farmer's wife.

We checked over the little Shadow to ensure that it was strongly tied down for the night before setting off for home, dropping Rob off at the airfield to pick up his car before I went off to Croydon to deliver the young lad back to his family. He loved the experience and, of course, he had had a long air experience and along with it, an adventure.

It had been a long day for me by the time I got home at about eleven o' clock that night—I was knackered.

The next morning, Rob and I flew to the farm in another Shadow and landed in the field. Both Shadows flew back to homebase, Redhill. Of course, once again the sun was shining: it was a lovely day.

Chapter Twelve
The Spanish Connection

During a visit from my private pension advisor and chitchatting with him afterwards, grumbling about the problem with running a Microlight Flying School in England—that being the number of times you couldn't fly because of the weather—he gave me the idea about moving the flying school to Spain where the sun shone all the year round. I must say, though; I then tried it twice with a few years in between attempts—an exhausting experience.

I didn't have much success at the first attempt, which started with a disaster. I set off with two elderly gentlemen, Jack and Ted. We took my old Mercedes, Shadow trailer in tow, and travelled to Bilbao by ferry—which seemed to take forever—three days in fact. Then, we drove down through Northern Spain, past Barcelona, then Valencia, to Benidorm where we intended to stay—the airfield a few miles away, being between Benidorm and Alicante.

Well, I can remember it was useless trying to share the driving. We had the twenty-two-foot trailer with an aircraft in it in tow. Jack just wanted to sleep, and Ted, whenever I got him to help me behind the wheel, kept moving the steering wheel slightly left, slightly right, left and right. When I asked him to stop as it was making us sick sitting in the passenger seats, he told me that he was used to driving his tractor which had play in the steering, and in order to drive the tractor straight, he had to take the play out of the steering by moving the wheel from left to right and right to left and he was used to the habit. So, even letting Ted drive was not painless.

After we had done most of the journey, though, we had food in the car. Ted refused any food offered to him, and he had eaten nothing. Because of his age (late seventies), I was very worried about that, so with only about two hours' driving left before we reached the end of our journey, I made one of the biggest mistakes of my life. We pulled into a 'Services' near Valencia. It was raining heavily, and we parked the car in a parking bay. All the parking bays were covered by corrugated sheet iron just as you see on bike sheds. The restaurant area was a little away from the parked area. I had my passport in the car, and with the car parked and passport in hand, I wondered whether I should keep the passport with me in my pocket—but then, instead, decided to lock it in the boot with all the luggage. That was a disastrous decision, as it turned out. We locked the car; the aircraft was attached to the car in the twenty-two-foot trailer which was locked—so that was OK.

As I followed the two old boys into the eating area, it was raining hard. On the way into the restaurant, I passed a small car, a Peugeot, parked with a young man behind the wheel. Strangely, there was another man sitting behind him in the back seat. I thought at the time, *why would a friend be sitting in the back seat?* We went inside and ate and then, to our distress, when we got back to the car, we discovered that we had been robbed. The thief had broken the driver's door lock, and in doing that, had automatically unlocked the boot of the Mercedes with all our luggage, mine and Jack's. Valuables including, you've guessed it, my passport, were all gone, all except Ted's old suitcase that was so old and tatty and tied up with string, that the thieves guessed there was nothing of value inside. I lost all the clothes that had been in my suitcase *and* all the important documents for the aircraft including my pilot's log books with proof of over three thousand hours of flying.

What a mess; and a lot of stress! Of course, the documents would have been worthless to the thieves but priceless to me. I also saw, while we were at the car with the Spanish police who came eventually, that there was another odd-looking character there in a beaten-up Volkswagen Dormobile. I suspect that he was the next shift of thieves waiting for another unsuspecting tourist! Of course, though we'd got the Spanish police involved, we had no chance of retrieving our stolen items. We carried on to our destination, but how I wish we had never stopped, for we now had a lot of work to do getting costly replacement entry papers that we would require for the homeward journey, even though they'd be snatched from us at the UK Border.

That was not the first time we drove all the way from the UK to the airfield in Spain. The next time, we took the Land Rover and there were four of us, including young Winston; and I had a plan to protect ourselves from these thieving bastards. This was the plan. First, when we stopped, we would select a well-lit service area and then two of us would go in for egg and chips (other food

109

was available) and two would stay with the Land Rover. Then we would swap. When I was guarding the Land Rover, I had a jack-handle in my hand for extra protection. Nobody was going to rob me again!

This worked well, and we had no problems, but when we drove back from Spain to England, we stopped at a service station in the Valencia area again. It was broad daylight, and the sun was bright. We didn't need fuel, but we wanted to use the toilet block. Two of us stayed outside with the Land Rover and, as the others came out, what we saw at the fuel pumps about 500 yards away, we couldn't believe. A man ran past the pumps with another chasing him, shouting something in Portuguese. A small car, with three young men inside, almost ran the first man down, but instead of helping, the back door opened, and in got the thief, before the car sped off at the service area exit, down the motorway. Yet another set of thieves! It turned out that we had just witnessed another robbery in action.

We later found out that the Portuguese man and his wife had driven into the services, the thief had snatched the wife's handbag through the open car-window—and run! I did not understand the language, but from the distress on the couple's faces, I would surmise that the wife had carried the passports and valuables in her, now stolen, handbag, as women do. A sad day, a poor reflection on human nature and an unpleasant thing to see—especially having been in the situation myself. I felt deeply for these Portuguese couple.

As we crossed the French Border, we stopped again, and while I was on duty guarding the Land Rover, jack-handle in hand, I noticed a Ford. 'People Carrier' stacked to the brim with suitcases visible through the back window. When I was relieved of guard duty and it was my turn to go in to eat, I believe I saw the owners of the people carrier—two young couples eating and drinking with no idea of the risk to their valuables and clothes on open view, from thieves who might be hiding in the long grass; and, of course, with thieves having mobile phones watching you eat, they can rob you unhindered.

Having had the experience of being robbed, you then hear many other stories of methods in use by thieves—for example, gassing tourists to keep them sleeping in their caravans and robbing them unhindered while this gas has put them into a deep sleep. The unique story that I heard related to caravaners: if you were eating in the service area, while one of the thieves watched you eating, another outside would give the tyre on your caravan a slow puncture. When you drove off, they would follow, waving you down like good citizens and even offering to help you with your wheel-change—this, while another thief broke into your caravan to steal all your valuables. Another example, I am saddened to say, of some very nasty people in this world.

The little airfield to which we were driving is (or was and probably still is) near El Campello, on the Costa Blanca. Manuel was the airfield manager. When I first met Manuel, who had a moustache which looked a little like that of that great Spaniard, Salvador Dali, my first impression of him was what a miserable airfield manager! That was because he seemed to complain a lot, and though he recognised that the international language in aviation is the English Language, Manuel insisted that when you flew at his airfield, you learnt and spoke Spanish. That said, the strange thing was, when you were in the circuit and a larger military aircraft was coming in and there was a safety issue, he would amazingly warn you over the radio in English, bless him! Anyway, as miserable as he seemed, he allowed us to fly from his little airfield with the long tarmac runway and liked and got used to him.

When we first arrived at the airfield, our business was slow to start. The airfield had a couple of offices, and, to its bonus, it had a cafe. A lot of our students and pilots came over to Spain to the airfield to fly, and with the glorious weather, the students progressed very quickly. However, it seemed to me that the Spanish had some peculiar ways. For example, the editor of an English-speaking newspaper told us that if the Spanish one day decided to change which side of the road to drive on, that is, from the right-hand side of the road to the left, the government would tell everyone *except* the most important people—the car drivers. This way of thinking was particularly frustrating when we returned a couple of years later. Sadly, then, we heard that Manuel had suffered a heart problem while under surgery and had died. We missed him as, while he was awkward to deal with, he seemed to have a kind heart.

When we returned, though, I did meet James, an elderly man, my friend who had helped us. Though he was English, he had lived in Spain for many years and could speak good Spanish. After I arrived at the Spanish Airfield, Mutxamel, someone had bought a flexwing microlight over from the UK to fly in Spain while its owner and his wife were on holiday. I did not meet the owner pilot, but James told me that he had flown a few times with the owner over the mountains. I asked James if there were many fields where they flew over the mountains. "None," he said.

Oh no! I had noticed that this man's flexwing microlight had the old type 'Rotax 447' engine, which had only the single ignition system and not the double ignition of later models—the same underpowered, unreliable engine that I had had on my first Shadow, the very same engine that had given me nearly all my engine failures! I told James this and advised him that mountain flying with a single ignition engine, when eighty percent of engine failures were caused by ignition faults, is not a good idea.

Later in time, I had, by this time, combined with another school, and we were ready to have another go at operating in Spain. We hoped and planned to fly both Cessna and microlight aircrafts from the airfield. However, the airfield had been changed drastically, as a big company, involved with helicopter maintenance, had bought the land and had erected a vast hangar.

Unfortunately, after that company had moved in, the new owners told a small Belgian company, which had been on the airfield for a very long time and which built fast 'Lancair' aircraft from kits, that they would only renew their lease to continue with their business for six months. This company had been on the airfield for many years: it couldn't continue with such a short lease, given so much uncertainty, because it was evident that that offer was tantamount to giving the company notice to quit. It was also *my* impression that this helicopter maintenance organisation would have loved to have got shot of the little Spanish flying school that had been on site for many years too—but Spanish law prevented removal of an historic tenant until he went of his own accord.

A good Spanish rule stipulated that if you rent a property for more than twelve months and the landlord decides to sell the property you, as the tenant, have be given first refusal to buy said property. I think that that rule applied to the little flying school.

It seemed that the helicopter company made things difficult for our flying club as well. This became apparent when, after our long negotiations with the club to use the facilities, along with satisfying the eleven members of its committee after many trips back and forward to Spain, we finally shook hands on an agreement. We would train with two Cessna aircraft to start, rent an office, pay to use the facilities, and all was going well. We even managed to rent a large villa that would accommodate the students' wives and families with a separate building for the instructors: and there was a swimming pool; and the villa even had the bonus of a few stray cats around complete with their kittens, all this within a short walk of the airfield.

We set a date to start the business and our students were there ready to fly, only to be told by the club chairman, on the day we got to the airfield to start, that the owners of the land had now come out of the woodwork and demanded that we pay them fifty euros per day, per aircraft to fly at the airfield! They left it until the start day to tell us this, which meant seven hundred euros per week plus the five hundred per month to the little flying club to add on for our students. This killed our project stone-dead as we had now been priced out of the market. Nobody would fly all the way to Spain and pay double the price for their flying lessons—even though the weather there was better. The only thing to do was to pack up and go home. After all that sweat and toil, our Spanish venture had flopped.

Of course, I had to go back—not to start another division of the flying school but to retrieve my Shadow aircraft and the old Range Rover parked in storage. The Shadow came back inside the trailer, and we recovered our Cessna 150 Aerobat which was flown back from Costa Blanca to Redhill. While we were licking our wounds, we concentrated on our Redhill operations.

Chapter Thirteen
Attention from 'The Powers That Be'

We were a small business, and I foolishly had engaged a large accountancy firm to do the accounts. The accountants were very good but costing a lot in high fees, so I went to chat to my bank manager. The manager recommended another, small accountant, whom I naturally assumed was professional and a chartered accountant.

I was pleased that we had a small accountant, because that had lowered our accountancy bill: apart from having to pay a couple of thousand pounds in corporation tax—which, I found out later, I didn't owe! Until I found that out, I was fairly happy. Unfortunately, that happiness did not last long!

I received a phone call from this accountant saying that the Taxman was looking at Cloudbase (as The Flying School was now named). "Was there a problem?" I asked but then got even more worried when he told me that he was going to get his friend, a chartered accountant, to look at the club's books.

"Are you not a chartered accountant?" I asked. Well, he was not, and worse, he later told the two men from the tax office, a Mr Slaughter and his sidekick, Mr Florence, that he had lost my books in a flood. It also appeared that the only reason for my company having been flagged was that this new accountant had changed an historic figure—the stock value—and the HMRC computer had flagged up the change. With this new figure, the bells had started to ring, and whistles had started to blow!

The mistake that I had made—yes, another one, foolish me again—was assuming that these tax men were nice people; the second mistake was agreeing to meeting them for interview. Not that I had anything to hide, but when I was asked about the closing stock figure, I had no idea what that was! Slaughter said, "You're the director; you should know." I explained to him that if I was not only a pilot but an accountant, I would not have had to employ an accountant at great expense as I would have done my own books. Unfortunately, not being an accountant myself did not do my argument any good, as I was told that, as director of the company, it was my problem; and my accountant, with his poor excuse of losing my books, was allowed to disappear into the sunset with no responsibility to me at all!

After my interview, Mr Slaughter and Mr Florence, another two men in the nasty club, decided that they would do a little research—all inaccurate, I may add; and after that flawed research, they concluded that I had earned an extra twenty-five thousand pounds per year. They kindly multiplied that by six as they are allowed to go back six years, on the assumption that earnings had been the same for each of those years, making one hundred and fifty thousand pounds, before finally dividing that by four and deeming almost thirty-eight thousand was what I owed Her Majesty's Revenue and Customs in unpaid corporation tax.

The investigation lasted two years, and my life was made a misery. Apart from the expense of finding a good accountant prepared to fight my case, I then had two girls come to see me regularly to present me first with a thousand-pound corporation tax fine unless I paid back my fictitious extra earnings by the month end, rising to two thousand if I couldn't and so on. I can now understand why some people have heart attacks or jump in front of trains.

My saviour was in my midst, though. I had taught him to fly. Though he flew like an eighteen-year-old in a sports car, Terry was a really good accountant— he was chartered and ran his own accountancy firm. Terry offered to look at the books. Of course, he now had to redo six years' worth of books, which, of course, cost me again for work previously done. But eventually, he proved that Mr Slaughter and Mr Florence were useless in their investigations and therefore, their calculations.

It appeared that Slaughter and Florence had sneakily contacted the airfield tower directly and been told how many landings we had done over the preceding year and then come to a financial conclusion that was completely wrong. At that time, we charged seventy-six pounds per hour for flying lessons, and when Redhill Tower told them that we had done, for example, two hundred landings, they proceeded to multiply that number by seventy-six, assuming that each landing was by a different student. Their mistake with that was failing to recognise that when a student gets to that part of the syllabus in which he or she practises landing the aircraft, that student could do many landings in that training hour and that therefore, each landing was definitely not by a different student.

Also, they had failed to recognise that some student pilots were shareholders in the aircraft, paying a much-reduced rate. In other words, their estimate of extra income based on one-landing-one-student was incompetent—and rubbish!

Terry called me to tell me that Slaughter and Florence had asked for a meeting with him, in response to which he told them that their appointment day was not convenient as his partner was off on that day. When Slaughter asked why Terry needed his partner to be there, he replied, "You come in twos, we have two. You come in threes, we have three." Evidently, Terry was familiar with taxmen, and this was why he told me I should never have seen these nasty men alone. Terry told me that contrary to owing Slaughter and Florence thirty-eight thousand, in fact, HMRC owed *me* three thousand in tax overpaid!

But Slaughter didn't want to pay me the three thousand pounds. Terry told me this was the deal, and this, when I heard it, made my blood boil. Slaughter said, "We owe your client three thousand pounds, but we don't want to pay him that." This was where the blackmail came in.

"We will cancel all fines and look at no more books if we can keep the three thousand pounds." Well! When I heard this, I blew my top and told Terry to tell them to get stuffed! But, when Terry told me that he paid his bookkeeper forty-five pounds per hour and that, to go over the other six years' books would be costly, his advice was that I lose the three thousand that those bastards now owed me.

I was so upset with the stress of the previous two years and the fact that after all that stress I had been blackmailed by HMRC that when Slaughter spoke with me on the telephone, I told him that in future, my P45 would be available for inspection at the Job Centre, who would now be paying my National Insurance, as I was giving up the business and signing-on as unemployed. This, I did, as I had at this time lost all interest in running a small business. I also told Slaughter that I hoped to see him and Florence in the unemployed queue behind me as, in my mind, they were incompetent. If they had been working for me and wasted two years of taxpayers' money by wasting time investigating someone with no outcome apart from misery to that person (me, in this case), I would have sacked them. After that phone call, Ted told me that Slaughter and Florence did not want to get anywhere near me and now preferred to deal with him alone. I wonder why?

The HMRC experience is not the only unhappy brush with officialdom. In my thirty-three years of training pilots, I have had four not-particularly-pleasant 'run-ins' with the civil aviation authority. I never ever had any problems with the authority regarding my engineer's licences, but once I started the flying school, that seemed to change. It would be easy to be critical of some people there—but then, one has to recognise that they are only doing the jobs that they are there to do—and I have met some nice, sensible, people there.

Some years ago, I had the privilege of teaching the chief pilot of British Caledonian Airways to fly the CFM 'Shadow', an aircraft which he had bought after he retired, and I was interested when Jim talked about the 'people in the Glasshouse'. Jim and his wife were lovely people, and they used to give us tea and cakes after we had inspected his Shadow aircraft for its annual Permit to Fly. But Jim had a very strong dislike of the people in 'the Glasshouse'.

At this point, I shall digress slightly to tell you a funny story about my interview tests, and the outcome from them, because I learnt over the years at British Airways, a few tips in doing exams as I had done many.

When I went to the CAA to be tested for a job as an Aviation Surveyor, a young lady put the multi-choice test paper in front of me with sixty questions, but there were only forty-five minutes in which to complete it. The clock started, and off I went. Now, the first bank of questions I studied and thought about and answered, but I was aware from past experiences that the tests are designed to test ability to work quickly against the clock—for example, you might spend lots of time on question 10, a complicated question and run out of time, only to find as you disappointedly hand back the exam paper that question 11 was a really simple question! Yes, in the past, I was caught out, too.

Well, the questions were getting harder and unrelated to the job, in my opinion. For example, you would be given the results of a number of years of students at a university: these students would have been of all ages and the multi-choice answers would ask which is right; did the students between the years 1965 and 1969 do better in English and Physics than students in 1970 to 1973. And then, they would ask whether the students of 1970–1973 did better in Geography than those or some other students. That was the sort of analytical brain teaser set in the exams, and I, on reading this type of question, was stuck, consuming time.

I was starting to sweat and sweat even more when I realised that I had wasted too much time on this complicated question. I looked at my watch and, to my horror, I was two-thirds into the allotted time with only twenty out of fifty questions finished! I decided to go to 'Plan B', which was to guess the answers to this question and the next fifteen questions. After all, I thought, drastic times needed drastic measures, and by the law of averages, on a choice of three answers, I had a thirty-three-and-one-third chance of getting the right answer.

After I had guessed the answers of these fifteen questions randomly, A, B, or C, I looked at my watch and saw that I was ahead of time—so, I spent some of the remaining time usefully, again thinking about the questions and, guess what? I completed all the questions on time, even having time to go back to check a few early answers.

Dead on time, the young lady came in with military precision to tell me to put my pen down and to hand over my paper. She looked and she said to me, "Wow, you have done well." She told me that the guy next door doing the same test had run out of time and only got halfway through the paper. I told her the truth, that I had guessed many answers. I think that she thought that I was just being modest; nice thought but that was not the case!

I did feel sorry for the chap next door as I had been there and done it. I had no expectation of passing that exam, and in line with CAA secrecy, I didn't get a direct result, but I must have passed, as I was asked to attend the next phase, an interview; and subsequently, I was offered the post.

Unfortunately, I did not accept the job as my wife had then had a cancer scare, and it would have been a bad time for moving abroad, which would have been likely to happen had I accepted it. Later in life, though, the CAA still controlled and occasionally disrupted my business and my ability to pay my mortgage. I began to understand why Jim called them, in an uncomplimentary way, 'The Men in the Glasshouse'—but, enough said about that!

Chapter Fourteen
The Excitement Starts

Going back, my very first student was Dean, who jointly owned his own 'Shadow' aircraft with a friend, Dan. Dean was a good student, and because friend Dan had a pilot's licence while Dean was learning with me, he picked up some things when flying with Dan. I didn't like flying Dean's aircraft, though; it was a bit cosmetically 'tatty'. The previous owner had constructed the aircraft from a kit and, while not doing a particularly good build, he had also made the mistake after painting it, of foolishly putting the aircraft in an oven to dry, as you would with a car following a respray. The trouble was that the wings and centre section were covered with a synthetic fabric that had a 'memory'. The correct way to tighten this fabric during the build was to apply gentle heat from an iron or a hot-air gun—and to be extremely careful as the heat is applied while watching the fabric tighten. Putting the aircraft wings in a hot oven did not do the aircraft and its fabric much good, the tight fabric starting to bend the wing ribs.

Anyway, when Dean was ready for his final test, I arranged it with an examiner, who had a school at an unlicenced field near the coast. The trouble was that the field was also shared by sheep which kept the grass short. We decided, as this was an unfamiliar field, to have a test run, flying to the field when no one was about, a day early and landing there so that Dean could become familiar with the field before his test. Well, that was the plan, anyway.

I remember vividly, sitting in the seat behind Dean in his little blue Shadow. We took off from Redhill and climbed away, heading towards the coast. Dean was flying well, and I was relaxed in the back, just a passenger, sightseeing; he was that good. I remember thinking how good his flying was and what a relaxed flight we were enjoying. After all, he was almost a pilot. Well, we had the airfield in sight and the sheep were there, grazing. The examiner was not there, but he had told me to fly over the field low and that the sheep would scatter, leaving it clear to land. So, that's what we did. I told Dean to do a low pass, get the feel of the field and then climb back to eight hundred feet, circuit height, and then we would set ourselves up for a nice landing. Well, that, too, was the plan.

Now, Dean's flying around the circuit was nice. We flew downwind, then onto base leg and then onto finals. All was good, the landing speed was spot on. I, sitting in the back, had my hands foolishly on my lap. We came over the fence, and all was looking good. We got to the stage where we were about to 'flare' to land, and that is where, instead of hitting the ground, we gently lift the nose of the aircraft and fly level to the ground at about three feet above, but instead, Dean decided not to flare but to crash the aircraft into the ground! The undercarriage collapsed, and the propellor behind us was still turning at idle power.

Each blade was slicing into the ground, and unfortunately, when we came to this abrupt stop, we couldn't turn the engine off. The crash-landing had dislodged two important ignition wires, and without them connected to Earth, the engine kept going and the propellor kept turning, slicing the ground. All we could do was wait until the fuel ran out—unless we could think of some other way to stop the engine! I decided to put the 'choke' full on to enrich the fuel-air mixture feeding into the engine and with the engine too rich on fuel, it spluttered and then eventually stopped.

"*What a pratt*, I thought, me being the instructor, too relaxed with my hands on my knees instead of not hovering over the controls during one of the most important stages of flight, the landing. This was another lesson that I would learn the hard way from bitter experience."

Well, that was a bad day, as now, we had to go home to get the trailer, return to dismantle the aircraft and recover it to Redhill for me to repair. It took many trips and many hours. Dean took it well, considering it was his aircraft. Anyway, we repaired and got the aircraft airworthy again; and Dean, after getting his landings right, became a pilot, on the road to gaining more experience.

One day, a young man took an air experience flight in one of our Shadows and then decided that he would like to carry on to become a pilot. Karl was what I would call a nice lad, a bit of a dreamy character though, so I knew teaching him would be a little bit taxing.

Every instructor will tell you that the money earned teaching, of course, goes towards paying their bills, but it is only a small part of teaching someone to fly. The fact is, you take that person, Karl in this instance, on as a project in that you want him to achieve his goal of getting his pilot's licence—but of extreme importance is the fact that you also want to teach him to be a very good pilot. You don't want him to kill himself—or his passengers, should he in future years choose to move on to another aircraft that may or may not be as forgiving as the Shadow microlight, which he is flying as a student.

Karl progressed satisfactorily until we got to the stage of training where I had to teach him how to land the aircraft. Landing an aircraft is the hardest part of training, and where, in Karl's case, we slowed right down to a snail's pace.

We had completed around 17 hours, so far, in 'the circuit', and Karl was still well short of landing the aircraft. My method of helping the student to land was to paint by numbers, so to speak In other words, I would talk the student down, with an instruction to obey my commands instantly. So, in reality, they were my hands on the controls, and if the student obeyed to the letter, I normally found that the student could land the aircraft five times out of five. However, I found with some students that you could find after many circuits, that rather than thinking for themselves as to when to 'flare' and how to hold the aircraft off the ground, they would just be lazy—not landing the aircraft but instead waiting for that next verbal command.

This phenomenon is similar to travelling somewhere using the Global Positioning System (GPS) in your car: you may have even repeated the journey more than once, but when you haven't got the GPS, you are lost because you never noticed landmarks when the GPS was directing you. This would be proved when I told the students to try a landing by themselves without my verbal help. That was when things normally went 'tits up' (to use the vernacular)!

Well, we were approaching 19 hours in the circuit, and Karl was getting very despondent at his inability to master the landing. I thought that it might be better to take him out of the circuit and do some normal flying instead, to give him a break from the intensity of the circuit. There was then, though, something that amazed me. Because Karl had done so many hours in the circuit, his general flying skills were excellent—so much so that when you asked Karl to fly at 1300 ft, you wouldn't get 1250 ft or 1350; you would get exactly what you had asked for he was that good. But of course, he couldn't land the bloody aircraft! Karl's height control was spot on but when back, practising crosswind landings, he was struggling!

I was helping him verbally to line up with the centre of the runway, but he kept drifting off. He was in the front seat; I was behind him in the back. In frustration that he was not getting it, I thought that I would try something new. The wind was coming from our left so we were 'crabbing' as we call it. In other words, the nose of the aircraft was pointing to the left into the wind so that the aircraft could maintain the (mentally) extended runway centreline. With the aircraft in this crabbed position, I told him to put a bit of his spit on his finger and then on the part of the windscreen that corresponded with the runway numbers. The spit ended up on the right-hand side of the windscreen, and then I told Karl to fly the aircraft so that the spit didn't move from the runway numbers, and eureka! He got it, but frustratingly, there was one other problem to solve with Karl.

Would sit in the back and think, *as we approach 'finals' to land, we were a bit high or sometimes, low.* I would wait as long as I could to see whether Karl would react but no, so I would need to say it, "We are a bit high, Karl, aren't we?" The reply was annoying.

"I thought that," Karl would say. On other occasions, the opposite would come in, with the farmhouse roof getting closer and closer. "We are a bit low Karl, aren't we?"

"I thought that!" he would reply, very annoyingly, as this happened time after time. Again, he evidently knew the problem but waited for someone else, that person being me, to notice and correct him. Very irritating!

Well, on the twenty-third hour of pounding the circuit, I had had enough. Karl was now landing the aircraft unaided albeit me having to tell him he was too high or too low, so I thought it was time that I got out and sent Karl off alone on his first solo flight. I told him that on the next landing, I was going to get out and that he was then going to go solo. After we landed, I exited the aircraft. It was difficult getting out of the back of the Shadow through the roll bars, but before I left Karl to his own devices, I told him, "Now, Karl, if you think you're too high, you're too bloody high! If you think you're too low, you're too bloody low!" I emphasised to him that I wouldn't be in the back to help him, and that he was on his own. The approach being high or low was down to him and this was my only worry.

I could do no more, but it seemed to do the trick. I walked back to the club as Karl taxied out. Karl did a nice circuit and then a very nice landing. I primed all the lads back at the club, telling them that Karl was flying alone. They all knew that the tradition was of great applause and congratulations to any pilot after a first solo, so when Karl had taxied back to the club after his momentous achievement, he could expect that traditional welcome. The only problem was that after Karl landed, he evidently forgot where he was and got lost! He started taxying in the wrong direction and was going not back to the club, but instead over to the far side of the airfield—and the rotten devils in Air Traffic Control waited until our student was almost on the road to Crawley before asking him where he was going!

Of course, the lads were hysterical with laughter—we all had a good laugh—but I did tell them not to let Karl see them laughing, for as far as I was concerned, bringing the aircraft down in one piece was enough for me. He could have taxied to Crawley after achieving that, for all I cared at that moment, for another pilot had been created.

One day, I flew with a friend from work, Alex. Alex was a trained pilot and had built a 'Europa' aircraft in his garage at home. We were flying the Shadow with its little 'Rotax 447' two-stroke engine, which had only one ignition system. Unfortunately, at this time, we did not have dual ignition on our engines then, so these little engines were not so reliable. We had decided to go from Redhill to look for a field in Guildford, where there was a farm where the farmer was a fellow microlight pilot—but we did not know exactly where this field was.

I was once again crammed into the back cockpit; Alex was flying the Shadow from the front seat. Everything was going fine until we got to Guildford, and then, the engineer in me listening to the engine thought that the engine note didn't sound quite right. I asked Alex to try to climb the aircraft, and when he applied more power, my suspicions were confirmed—the engine would not accelerate but started to misfire and the aircraft wouldn't climb. As Alex increased the power to climb, the engine spluttered and lacked power. The most we could do was to maintain height or descend, and the engine now sounded a little rough.

As luck would have it, when we looked below for a suitable field in which to land, to our surprise, there was a man on the ground holding an orange windsock. We had found our microlight man with his farm just in the nick of time, by the look of it!

We worked out the wind direction from the windsock and performed a good landing on his farm. The farmer told us that he had heard our rough-running engine and quickly gone to get his windsock to show us the direction in which to land. We landed safely.

The fault was simple to fix—a broken earth wire to the ignition, which meant that the engine had been running on only one cylinder, with not enough power to allow that small, thirty-eight-horsepower, two-stroke engine, to keep us flying. Our new friend lent us some tools, and we fixed the broken earth wire, had a cup of tea and a chat, and, mission accomplished, thanked our new friend before our little Shadow climbed into the sky on its way back to Redhill Aerodrome.

Following another very satisfactory training flight, my student, Simon, and I were returning from the lesson in our CT. The weather was good and the skies clear. We called Redhill to rejoin from the local landmark, Bough Beech Reservoir, and we were told to go to Godstone to rejoin the circuit to land on runway 08 left. We got to Godstone and started to join the circuit 'downwind'. Each circuit at an aerodrome is divided into an imaginary rectangle. The section parallel to the runway in use, and with the wind pushing the aircraft from behind, is called 'downwind'. As we entered the downwind leg, I saw a bird of prey—a big buzzard—coming towards us fast, but he was much higher than the 1200 ft at which we were flying, so I was only a little concerned.

Simon was flying the aircraft. He was in the left seat. I alerted him to the bird heading towards us and said, "Give me control." I pushed the control column forward, which lowered the nose of the aircraft into what amounts to a dive. In this aircraft, a 'CT', this action gave a lot of height clearance between us and the buzzard. *Collision avoided—or so* I thought. The buzzard, though, instead of flying over us as I had expected, decided to dive and attack this strange-looking white bird, the CT! The buzzard flew through the propellor and straight through the Perspex windscreen, hitting Simon in the face, cutting his lip and giving him a black eye. After that attack, I looked across to Simon, and with the perfect buzzard-shaped hole in the screen, the bird ended up dead just behind Simon's neck. It was as though he was wearing a scarf!

I pressed the 'transmit' button and told Frank in the control tower that we had had a bird-strike, and I requested an ambulance—especially as, from my seating position, I couldn't see Simon's left eye. I was hoping that he still had it!

We landed safely, and Simon got the care of the paramedics. Luckily, the Air Ambulance operates from Redhill Aerodrome and once checked, Simon had no serious injuries, just a black eye and a cut lip. When we retrieved the poor buzzard from the aeroplane, we noticed that the propellor had chopped off his tail. Later, I thought how lucky we were that the buzzard had died instantly, as a wounded bird flying around our small cockpit would have made my landing very difficult.

the event, Simon said when the buzzard came in the cockpit, he was dead worried that I was incapacitated, meaning he would have had to land the aircraft, but luckily, I was in the better seat on this occasion. I remained uninjured.

Talking about unexpected travellers in the aircraft, on a previous occasion, years earlier, after I had got airborne with a student, I soon noticed that we had an uninvited passenger in the cockpit, a wasp. I hate wasps! There is always a high risk of being stung by them and they tend to pester you, but while thinking about our extra passenger, I didn't mention it to my student. After all, I didn't want to disturb his concentration and, in any case, we couldn't open a window or get him out—so I stayed quiet, resigned to the fact that I might get stung—but much better to fly the aircraft than lose control because of a wasp sting! Luckily, the wasp seemed to realise that he was not in a normal place and settled, slightly subdued I thought, up by the wing root, well out of our way and staying out of the way all through the flight. Once landed, I opened both doors and let him escape into the sun while we went for a coffee.

The buzzard—though not the wasp—added to my 36-year teaching record during which time of fourteen engine-out landings, three near-misses with other aircraft, two bird strikes (in the previous strike, the bird hit the wing after take-off) and lastly, an electrical fire more recently.

Chapter Fifteen
The Excitement Continues

One beautiful flying day, one of our shareholder pilots announced that his friend, who had a field next to his house, had invited him to fly the Shadow there to play cricket. I asked Colin, the shareholder pilot, what the field was like for its suitability to land an aircraft.

"My friend says it is perfect!" he said.

"How long was it, and what was the surface like?" I asked.

"It's all good," was the enthusiastic reply!

Jim, one of my other instructors, also asked Colin the same questions, also asking if he had ever walked the field. He had not walked, or even seen, his friend's field, but it was all good, he stated emphatically.

Well, he set off from Runway 26R in the Shadow with a full tank of fuel, climbed into the clear blue sky and disappeared from sight. After an hour or so, we of course got the dreaded telephone call from Colin. He had tried to land the aircraft in his friend's field but, contrary to what he had previously thought, in fact, this field was a very rough field, devoid of flatness. Colin told us that the nose wheel had dug in and been ripped off.

Then, of course, Colin told us that he had had to leave to get to the cricket match; after all, a crash-landing in someone else's aircraft was not going to spoil that, and so, requested that *we* sort out the aircraft—as you do, when you are a stockbroker and used to members coming out to recover the aircraft and clean up your mess! After all, we couldn't disrupt the cricket match, could we?

When I got there, I couldn't believe the state of the field. It had evidently been used for grazing cattle—and recently; and with me having had polio and having a dodgy, slightly curved right foot that is not flat, I kept tripping over the footprints made by the cows' hooves. It was terrible! I would have been nervous bringing our Land Rover into that field, let alone trying to land a microlight aircraft.

That was an expensive cricket match for the flying school!

On one of my few days off, I went shopping in Brighton with my girlfriend. During the afternoon, I received a telephone call from Steven—yes, the same Steven who flew back in forty knot winds, now one of my instructors who was running Cloudbase for the day in my absence. He told me that aircraft shareholder Neville and one of the club members had landed our Jabiru aircraft in a field near Bromley. They had made a precautionary landing as they had thought that the engine was a little low-powered. I took my girlfriend home and off I went to find our 'Jabiru', our aircraft in this field, apparently full of cows, near Bromley.

The cows were very interested in the Jabiru, and this was disturbing as I knew, cows chew on aircrafts that are not made from metal: so, leaving the aircraft overnight and finding it eaten by morning was not an option. I had stopped at the airfield to collect Matt, who then accompanied me on our trip. We eventually found the field, and after removing the top engine cowling, I quickly found the problem: the carburettor heat valve, which pilots use during flight to remove any ice which may have formed in the carburettor venturi tube and especially when landing, would not work properly. A spindle, which turns a metal disc valve to 'open' or 'close' hot airflow that comes from the engine exhaust jacket when selected by the pilot, had become detached from the disc, so that the disc didn't move when the spindle did.

The heat valve was set in the hot position, which gave the engine a reduction in power. I temporarily fixed the problem but then, I needed to fly the aircraft out of the field and back to Redhill. The curious cows were looking with interest at the group of people around the strange object that had invaded their space. We also had an audience of people looking over the hedge. I decided to walk the field to get an idea of length and the surface and slope. Take-off would be slightly downhill, and the aircraft was light—but the field, of course, was grass, which retards the aircraft on its take-off (or landing) run there was also trees at the end of the field.

Matt asked me if I wanted a passenger, but I told him that it would be best if I flew alone for weight reasons and best for him to take the car back with the two pilots, and I am really glad that I did. I 'ran up' the aircraft engine, selected flaps to the take-off position and 'wound up' the engine on the brakes at the very end of the field, holding it at full power, then I released the brakes. As I let the brakes go, our Jabiru started to accelerate along the field, heading towards the trees at the far end. The grass was holding the aircraft back, but eventually, the little Jabiru left the ground. With the trees approaching, I lifted the nose a little more. The engine was at full power, the day was warm, and the wind was light—not a good combination for even a light aircraft taking off: a stronger wind on my nose would have been better. The stall-warner just started to beep so that was the limit for lifting the nose: I was getting the maximum lift from the wings.

The trees were getting closer and closer, and I was starting to sweat, but phew! I cleared them, and I set a course for Redhill Aerodrome. Once I'd got the aircraft up, it was a nice flight. The boys were driving my car back to Redhill, and best still, the cows would be disappointed in that our little Jabiru would not be their meal for the night!

One thing, though: after I had taxied the Jabiru back to the hangar, having arrived at Redhill and got out, there was a bit of tree greenery on one of the wheels; and when we were having a cup of tea, I did think, *thank God I did not have young Matthew sitting with me in the passenger seat*, as things certainly could have, some would say, been very different!

Then, there was the 'Episode of the Scottish Loch'. An old colleague at British Airways, now an insurance broker, telephoned me to say that his company had a 'Rotax 503' engine that had been removed from a Shadow that had been submerged in a Scottish Loch. He said that the engine had been stripped—in other words, it was in bits in a box—and he asked whether I was interested in having the box of bits. I was intrigued to know the story of the aircraft to which it had belonged. All that my friend knew was, that apparently, the aircraft—another Shadow—had suffered an engine failure and had landed in the water in one of the Lochs in Scotland. The aircraft was found to be a total loss when recovered: this was the engine from that aircraft.

I cleaned the crankcase halves, fitted a new crankshaft and pistons and overhauled the little '503'. My friend told me that the cause of the failure had never been found. Luckily, the little Shadow floats, so the pilots escaped unscathed. We, at our club, had five Shadows, and we had extra engines. The advantage of this was that we had another engine readily to hand, an overhauled engine to fit when one needed to be serviced. That involved stripping and rebuilding the little two-stroke. Maintaining a current logbook for each engine meant that each Shadow could be back in service straightaway after its engine had been swapped.

Well, the Scottish Loch engine—let's call it 'Nessie', as it turned out to be a monster—acted true to form and failed again, burning a hole in the aft piston, and then, annoyingly after many flying hours following repair, failed again—making a hole in the same piston again! We were running out of ideas. We knew that the hole was caused by the engine suddenly running with a lean fuel-air mixture and that that caused a hot spot, and burning the hole, but we were scratching our heads to find the cause.

During one engine stripdown, I unintentionally swapped the front cylinder head with the rear cylinder head, and that was when we had a stroke of luck, albeit that we still holed another piston! While running the engine, suddenly, the problem moved from the rear cylinder to the front cylinder—the piston that was being holed was now in the forward cylinder, indicating that something in that cylinder head was burning holes in pistons.

On close examination of the offending head, and very difficult to see, it appeared that at some stage, someone had evidently stripped the thread of the spark plug. The previous owner, I guess, had, probably, taken the head to a local engineering firm for repair, and the engineers had made a beautiful steel insert that screwed into the head. Then, the spark plug screwed into the insert. It looked a professional job and was almost invisible—it looked so good—but we found that the insert, being made from steel while the cylinder head was made from aluminium, became loose in the aluminium head when hot because of the different rates of expansion of the two metals as they heated up. Eureka!

As the cylinder head temperature increased to its normal running temperature, the insert, being made from steel and expanding more slowly than the aluminium cylinder head, became loose so that the piston was able to suck air into the cylinder through the gap between the fitting and the cylinder head. This made the fuel-air mixture weak and pow! Another hole in the piston. A small engineering mistake had caused the loss of a perfectly good aircraft in the Scottish Loch.

Now, I will tell you how I met young Matthew. We met schoolboy Matt over the flying school's 36 years in existence. The Flying School and Club had many requests from youngsters who wanted to come to work and to help out in return for the chance to learn about the aircraft and flying and to have the occasional flight with a club member—or, better still, to have a proper lesson with a flying instructor. We asked them to do little jobs like cleaning the aircraft and to help out: in return, they could have a flight. However, we had in the past a bit disappointed with some of the 'helpers' because they did more flying with club members than they did work—so we had to stop them coming to the club.

One of our instructors asked if he could bring in his next-door neighbour's lad to get some work experience. I said yes, but this time, we had a foolproof plan to get the young lad, Matt, who was fifteen, to clean five aircraft with one of us inspecting each aircraft after it had been cleaned. We would sign a chit, and when Matt had five signed chits, we would give him an hour's instructional flying.

Matthew was a nice lad and very enthusiastic. He soon fitted into the team and became one of the active club members, progressing with his flying quickly as he was a keen 15-year-old. Often, I would come to work only to find him already cleaning one of our aircrafts without being asked, this before anyone else had arrived. Even though Matt had completed his training, he had to wait to get his licence through the post as the CAA held on to his application until his seventeenth birthday. (A student pilot may count hours and log them from age 14 and can fly solo from age 16—but may not acquire a licence until aged 17).

On his birthday, licence in hand, he was interviewed by a reporter for his local newspaper with the headline in the paper 'Schoolboy Can Fly Before He Can Drive!' Almost 15 years later, he now flies an Airbus for 'Easyjet' and still flies for us too, completing 'air experience' flights using his skills; and, he has remained my friend and one of the team.

"'Our English man who lived mostly in Japan' was a gentleman from whom I had a phone call, telling me that he had just bought an aircraft and asking if we could teach him to fly it. It turned out that the aircraft was not like the Shadow microlights or the Jabiru that we flew at this time. In fact, it turned out that the aircraft was a very early flexwing microlight called a 'Charghus Titan'. The flexwing is a fabric, delta wing, aircraft. Attached to the wing is a pod which holds the two pilots side by side and the engine and propellor."

On the Charghus, like many other flexwings, the one bolt that attached the wing to the pod was aptly named the 'Jesus' bolt—the reason being that you were extremely likely to meet your maker if this bolt failed!

The story was that the elderly British gentleman had spent part of his time living in Japan, and he had purchased this aircraft from an insurance company after the Charghus factory had gone into liquidation. The insurance company had acquired the assets which included this new, unfinished aircraft.

The aircraft, in particular, was very strange. It had two seats side by side, inside an apex frame of aluminium tubes. Inside this frame, there were two padded seats with no cockpit around them. Now, I wasn't used to two seats side by side or flying with no pod around them. A real aerial motorbike! I think if you weren't belted in, you would certainly fall out of the aircraft in a turn!

Well, there was another slight problem. While Asim, our instructor, was eager to the teach our elderly gentleman to fly, we had in fact to finish building the aircraft, which involved changing a few things, getting a Permit to Fly and doing a flight test. Unfortunately, when we contacted the Chief Engineer at the British Microlight Aircraft Association, we found out that there were modifications that we also needed to do to get the Permit to Fly—and there were many. We had to strengthen the wing tubes, replace structural cables for stronger ones, replace fuel system tubes and lots more.

Once we had completed the work, the next problem was to decide who was to do the test flight for its Permit to Fly after all none of us flew flexwing aircraft, but there was a name that came to mind—Donald, a man who had his own flexwing microlight and who loved flying flexwings. Also, he was not far from us in Kent.

I called him up, and he was game for testing this early flying motorbike. He told me that he would, with his friend, Eddie, who was a Check Pilot and who also flew flexwings for pleasure, would do the test flight—though, during his normal working day, he flew something much bigger: Captain Edward flew Boeing 747 jumbo jets for a living.

Amazing how when flying is in your blood, you can enjoy one day flying a Jumbo jet and the next day fly a little low-powered microlight.

The day had come. We packed up the Charghus and drove to Donald's airfield, put the aircraft together and gave the little 'Robin' engine a run after filling the fuel tank with two-stroke mix. The little Robin engine was brand-new, so it ran well. It had no gearbox, so the propellor was driven directly, by a thick belt wrapped around one pulley on the engine to another driving the propellor. In later engine designs, the drive belt was the first thing to be discarded as, if it were to snap, the propellor would stop spinning and the engine would overspeed breaking the engine, so the drive belt was the weak link. Newer engine designs gave us a gearbox to drive the propellor and two ignition systems which was altogether much safer.

Donald and Eddie took charge. They were both dressed for warmth in their 'Ozee' flying suits. You see, that's another problem with flying flexwings: apart from the fact that they do not have a rudder or ailerons, or in fact any conventional flight controls, flying in the wind without a shield from the wind made you bloody cold, even on a hot day when you were roasting in these flying suits while on the ground, once airborne without them, you would be freezing.

Well, before Don and Eddie set off, I told them the story of the aircraft and what we had to do to make it airworthy. I also told them at the start, because of all the work completed, to use caution and fly the aircraft gently. Well, that last instruction evidently went in through one ear and out through the other as, to my surprise, the aircraft leapt from the ground and flew like a sports car in the sky. I had my mouth wide open most of the time. Up and down, left and right, around behind me, then in front of me, the two aviators crisscrossed the blue sky, and after a long flight, I saw the Charghus wheels touch down in the grass field. Then, the little aircraft landed—and up it went into the blue sky again, before it touched down on the grass for what I thought was the final landing of the day.

"How was it?" I asked, and with that, Eddie handed me a crash helmet and I knew what that was for. There was no argument. It was evidently my turn to make sure that my engineering was up to scratch, as it was evident that I was going to occupy the passenger seat for the next flight!

Once I was strapped in, I told Eddie that I wasn't being overfriendly, but asked if me being in the right seat, he minded me wrapping my left hand around this bloody big pole that attached both of us to the wing above, just for my peace of mind—for I was a normal conventional aircraft instructor, used to an aircraft all around me with the luxury of a cockpit and a canopy that came over my head—unlike the Charghus which was, in fact, just two seats bolted to an aluminium 'A' frame with two people belted into those seats whistling through the air with two people strapped to them, only stopped from falling out by these seatbelts! A flying motorbike in reality, this was.

Well, I did enjoy it, but let's say I was glad to get out and see Earth under my seat when we landed. Not a flexwing pilot, me.

I asked Eddie afterwards if he would kindly write a brief Pilot's Operating Manual, as we didn't have one, stating various speeds and how the aircraft handled, so we could keep this with the aircraft and pass it on to my instructor and his student, the elderly man who had lived in Japan. Eddie told me that the Charghus was not a student's aircraft, but it was safe.

Sadly, those first flights of the Charghus were the last, certainly with us, as the elderly man never did learn to fly. His situation changed and he went back to live in Japan permanently, and instead, we just used the Charghus like a sand yacht without putting its wings on, until I gave it away to another aircraft inspector some years later. But I was glad that we proved it could fly, even though we did just the three flights. It is to be hoped that under the inspector's ownership, the Charghus 'Titan' is still taking to the air as I write.

We had a few airline pilots with us in the flying club apart from Eddie and young Matt. Captain Max Lowrey had a motorhome which he parked next to our old redundant caravan and slept in. When he had a flight next day from Gatwick, it saved him the travelling from his home in Cornwall, and he loved to fly our Cessna Aerobat when he was not flying the airliners for work.

He wanted to take me up in the Cessna to do some spinning, and of course, when he asked me, I always put it off with the response, "Yes, Mike, some other time." Well, that excuse could only last for so long and, sure enough, one day, when the weather was good and I turned the corner at the club, Capt. Max was sitting there with many other club members, and as soon as I rounded the corner Max said, "Good day for spinning!"

Let me explain before I progress that there are two things you do not want to do in normal flying and that is stalling and spinning—unless you are practising these manoeuvres and have plenty of height in which to recover. The reason for practising these exercises is so that you can get out of a dangerous situation, were you ever to stall an aircraft inadvertently, or get into a spin. The Civil Aviation Authority does not want instructors to practise spins with students because, in years past, when 'spinning' was an exercise that *was* practised, students and newly qualified pilots had many deadly accidents practising by themselves. Because of that, we don't now practise, and haven't for many years practised, spinning the aircraft in pilot training. Instead, we 'brief' students about spinning and recovery. (However, instructors are taught spinning and recovery as part of their training but not in microlights, I may add).

A spin is entered from a stall. The stall occurs when the aircraft is manoeuvred so that the wing loses lift—in other words, when the smooth airflow (known as laminar flow) over and under the wing, which provides lift to the wing, is disturbed. In particular, the smooth flow above the wing's trailing edge

133

is completely broken up, and it breaks away from the surface of the wing, causing the aircraft to lose height as the ratio of lift to weight of the aircraft, and its load is lost and the weight exceeds the lift generated by the wings. The aircraft descends like a brick.

The conditions needed for stalling are that either the aircraft is going too slowly, so that the airflow over the wings slows and can't flow over the leading edge of the wing, or the nose of the aircraft is raised to a very steep angle—a bit like pointing the nose upwards like the space shuttle—and once again, the airflow is disturbed and can't flow over the wing surface without breaking away. Practising the stalling exercise at a sufficiently safe height is part of learning to fly and so, part of practical pilot training. The spin can develop from a stall— essentially, when one wing drops relative to the other—so we need to know how to stop a spin and recover to normal flight; and we learn this in the classroom.

The spin occurs when one wing stalls before the other so, for that instant, you effectively have a one-winged aircraft, and the aircraft enters a spiral in the low wing direction at a very low airspeed. This is even more dangerous than the stall when close to the ground, as you might not have time or height to recover to normal flight. So, the spin can develop soon after you have stalled. What you definitely do *not* want to do is enter a stall, intentionally or unintentionally, close to the ground—say, when you are in the circuit and you're getting ready to land.

Well, technical stuff over and back to my having turned the corner to be confronted with about fifteen members of my club drinking coffee with Max and, once again, putting me on the spot, asking me once again to go up and practice spinning and recovery from the stall and spin. Well, what else could I do, confronted with such a situation in front of all those club members? And of course, as the chief flight instructor, I had to agree and look enthusiastic about it—and so I put on the false smile.

Now, embedded in my mind was the experience that I'd had with Asim my flight instructor way back when I was a student learning to fly the Cessna. He had decided to do stalling in weather, which I can only say was 'iffy' with local thunderstorms and strong winds—so much so that nobody else was flying. I remember too, the aircraft—a Cessna 152. I can remember the registration burnt into my memory: 'Whisky Papa' as, to my initial horror, on this Cessna, the wing always dropped aggressively when it stalled.

On the first stall that we did, when the speed decayed the right wing stalled before the left wing, so we had a one-winged aeroplane so to speak, and the aircraft rolled to the right aggressively. That spooked me, the student, that did, with Asim laughing, while he pushed the control stick forward, re-balanced the aircraft (i.e., ensured that the balance ball on the instrument panel was centred) increased power and took control.

"Have another go," he said, and after that initial shock, I was ready for it. I adopted an aggressive response, and I was in control of the situation after three goes. I was not spooked anymore—that was, until I noticed Asim at the moment of the stall shoving in a bit of left rudder to aggravate the situation, and that it did! While I was ready for another aggressive right wing-drop, the bloody aeroplane rolled aggressively to the left.

"That got you," said Asim, laughing out loud.

I had, of course, expected the normal right roll, but the lesson was learnt and never forgotten. I had seen it, done it and from that day, I became 'Phil the ever ready'. The experience, though, and the characteristics of that Cessna, remain forever in my memory.

Asim went on to fly for an airline and became an even more experienced pilot. I was hoping that my Cessna Aerobat, 'Golf Bravo Foxtrot Sierra' (G-BTFS), would be different and docile with no surprises like Whisky Papa, especially whenever we were going spinning!

Anyway, Max found some uncontrolled airspace and we flew at five thousand feet, well high enough for our spinning and recovery exercise. He throttled back, raised the nose of the aircraft, the airspeed decayed below 40 knots and as the aircraft stalled, Max shoved in a boot-full of left rudder. Off she went into a spin to the left. The exercise was that we would recover after we had let the aircraft spin three times—and so we did. Max put in opposite rudder, right rudder to stop the spin, as we were spinning to the left, then—when the spin had stopped, he 'neutralised' the controls (that is, returned them to their central flying positions) eased out of the dive, pushed the control column forward to lower the nose—and applied power so that the aircraft flew normally again.

Now, it was my turn. My recovery wasn't as good as Max's, but it was OK. We practised spinning to the left and to the right, and the aircraft did what we asked of it with no surprises, and was safe. I was pleased. It is always good to know your aircraft!

On the way back to Redhill, I asked Max if we could do a stall in the landing configuration, with flaps at thirty degrees, as I had done with Whiskey Papa many years earlier; and then, to try with flaps at forty degrees—the flap setting which my aircraft had but WP did not have. (The Cessna 150, predecessor to the Cessna 152, has flaps that can be extended to a maximum extension of 40 degrees: the Cessna 152 has flaps which extend only to a maximum of 30 degrees—a design change made, as I understand it, because the Cessna 150 with 40 degrees of flap extended required a very high power setting to be flown, and it was said that that had caused several accidents when approaching to land—the aircraft had been flown too slowly and stalled).

I was ready for any aggressive wing-drop, either right or left, but to my pleasant surprise, both wings stalled together—with no wing-drop and so, no surprises! At flaps thirty, the aircraft's behaviour was the same as for a stall with flaps at forty degrees, so I was well pleased! My aircraft was a good'un—and, of course, when we returned to Redhill, my fearless reputation remained in the eyes of the club members.

Unfortunately, there was a sad conclusion to this flying trip which brought back bad Spanish memories and that was that when Max had returned to his motorhome which he had parked in the car park while we flew, some bastard had broken in and robbed him, taking his suitcase with all his clothes and flight bag, which contained his commercial pilots licence and passport. Max was on flying duty the next morning, rostered to fly to Spain, and without his credentials, mainly his licence and passport, he had to call work and cancel all his flights until he could get a replacement passport and licence and sort out his personal possessions. I did wonder if those nasty people who robbed me in Spain earlier had followed us to Redhill. Food for thought. A sad, miserable end to an enjoyable flying experience.

Chapter Sixteen
And So It Goes On!

Years later, Steven—he of the windy day saga that I mentioned earlier but by now a better pilot—became one of our club's flying instructors. (One might say, "He learnt about flying from that.") One day, when we arrived at the airfield, the five Shadows were covered with snow. This happened many times in the winter, and we would sweep the snow off the wings with a soft yard brush and use a de-icing fluid, warm the aircraft up and get going. Steven was always so slow to get the aircraft ready, always last, then eventually, he would get the student strapped in at the front, start the engine with the pull starter and then haul himself through the roll bars to the back seat, belt himself in and close the canopy. It was, for us, like watching paint dry. Then, at last, when instructor Jim and I thought that he was off, we'd hear the engine stop again, the rear canopy open and Steven would haul himself through the anti-roll bars and out of the back seat. "What is wrong?" we asked.

"I have forgotten my gloves!" he would reply. That was Steven. There was also a good reason why we called him bicycle clips: he would cycle to the airfield but then would attempt to climb into the rear cockpit of the Shadow, his customer in the front, still with his bike clips on; he had forgotten to take them off!

On one occasion, we had arranged for our examiner to come to test three students. This was the students' final flying test, called the General Flying Test. Once this test was passed, they could apply for their long-awaited pilot's licences. Steven had been doing most of the pilot training in particular, flying with a student—a librarian, Colin. We did have students of all sorts. Colin appeared slightly eccentric, another quiet person. Yes, you wouldn't be surprised at him being a librarian—it fitted his character.

Colin was one of those students booked to do his test. With the examiner coming the next day, though, Steven announced to me that previous evening, "Well, of course. Colin is no good at engine-out landings."

"What?" I said. "He is doing his General Flying Test tomorrow!"

Oh, God! The day before his test, he was already destined to fail as, to pass the test, he must be able do one of the most important parts of the syllabus (amongst others)—the ability to glide the aircraft to a safe landing in a field if the engine stopped. Well, I took Colin to one side and spent 30 minutes briefing him on forced landings. Then, I insisted that we fly that afternoon so that he could show me what he could do in the event of this emergency.

Colin and I took a Shadow aloft, and I found a couple of suitable fields below and in front of us. Without a word to Colin, I pulled the throttle to idle and shouted to him, "Engine failure, you have control."

Even with these good fields available, Colin did nothing, so I said, "Colin, what is the plan?" He was dumb; and worse, he did nothing. So, I took back control and we returned to Redhill.

I told Colin I was not going to embarrass the good reputation of the school by presenting him to the examiner for test the following day when he was not ready. He evidently would fail in that he could not demonstrate the ability to land safely in a field if the engine stopped. This exercise was a very important one in the syllabus, because engine failure could happen, and we had to practise making it an inconvenience rather than a life-threatening incident. After all, microlight aircraft do glide. I, therefore, had no choice but to pull his name off the list for his General Flying Test that very next day.

I then overheard him repeating what I had told him to another club member, telling the other student pilot that I had stopped him doing his test with the others who were set to do theirs. After hearing that, I told Colin that I would give him one last chance, that I would brief him again on the exercise before he went home and that he was to come in early the next morning to fly with me at 0900 hrs when the airfield opened. I told him that before we flew, I would brief him again, and then I would demonstrate the manoeuvre myself once airborne. Then, he would have a go and that, subject to his performance on that early morning flight, I would decide whether to slot him in as Number Three for his General Flying Test. I did emphasise that him sitting in the front cockpit of the Shadow after I had simulated the engine failure and doing nothing was not an option!

Well surprise, surprise; I was impressed. I guess that he was a bookworm, being a librarian. I suspect that he had been studying the procedure all night, and it did the trick: we weren't embarrassed. On the contrary, he was now pilot material, and he passed his test later that day! As I said, everybody is different—you never know what they are going to do.

On the same day that Colin took and passed his General Flight Test, Wesley, a very good student, was booked in to do his General Flying Test. He was scheduled to do his test after lunch as again, one of the three tests on that day. At lunchtime, we all stopped for a break and went to the local pub for lunch with the examiner in tow. I heard Christine, who bought the drinks, shout across the bar, "Who is this whisky for?"

Amazingly I watched as Wesley's hand stretched out to grasp the whisky shot glass. Now, nobody who is about to fly should be drinking alcohol. (The maxim is eight hours between bottle and throttle—and that's a minimum time, and in fact, the alcohol level for flying is almost nothing). Before Wesley could lift the whisky to his lips, I asked, "What are you doing? I can't let you do your test if you take one sip of that!"

"I thought it would calm my nerves," Wesley replied. *Unbelievable!* I thought. *God give me strength!* What I also found out later was that the examiner with us in the pub was also watching the whisky glass as intently as I was. He told me later that one sip from that glass of alcohol would, of course, have meant Wesley's instant failure of the test, even before it started! Well, Wesley passed his test without any alcohol passing his lips, and he became a good pilot.

That said, Wesley did let the side down sometime later: by now, a very experienced pilot, he flew a Shadow a long distance—from Redhill to Compton Abbas in Dorset. The Shadow's fuel tank has only two hours' endurance. I told him that the wind would be against him on return from Compton to Redhill, and so, to top up the fuel tank at Popham, an airfield which he would pass close by, on the way back but also fairly close to Compton Abbas.

It always amazes me how some pilots value their money over their lives, and I suspect that Wesley could not justify to himself picking up as little as a gallon of fuel after only thirty minutes in the air en route back to Redhill—and having to pay a ten-pound landing fee as well, which would make it a costly gallon of fuel! So, instead of that, he decided to try to get back to Redhill without stopping.

Wesley got as far as Dorking in the stronger headwind before the aircraft engine spluttered and the aircraft ran out of fuel. What was going through his mind when he saw the fuel gauge needle flickering just above empty, I can only imagine—or maybe he didn't even look at the fuel gauge. I know that had it been me, I would have been sweating like a pig, watching the needle getting closer and closer to empty! Luckily for him, his flight training paid off, even though common sense was lacking, and he landed in a field near Dorking. Lucky for him, neither he nor the Shadow was damaged, otherwise a big repair bill would have followed. Nevertheless, a severe telling-off was necessary and well-deserved.

Now for a little bit of technical stuff. An aircraft flying has airspeed which, as the name suggests, is the speed of the aircraft *relative to the airflow past it*. The difference between airspeed and windspeed gives us the aircraft groundspeed (speed over the ground). If we are flying at 70 knots against a wind of 20 knots our speed over the ground, or groundspeed, is 50 knots. If we fly at an airspeed of 70 knots and the wind is pushing from behind, we have a groundspeed of 90 knots.

You can see that with a two-hour fuel endurance, if the wind had been behind Wesley on the way back, he would have made it back to Redhill without stopping as he would have been pushed by the added tailwind, making his groundspeed faster than his airspeed—but he made two mistakes: the wind was not with him but against him; and even had the wind been behind him, he should have filled up at Compton prior to return for peace of mind and landed to top up at Popham en route. Although that would have been an expensive option—just one gallon of fuel purchased and the added cost of a ten-pound landing fee—that nevertheless would have been the safe thing to do and the correct action to take, for running out of fuel cannot only be disastrous but is also an offence. It is if your car runs out of fuel on a motorway, and so is even worse when you are airborne, have lost your engine power and, because of your stupidity, not done your calculations and are now trying to land a gliding aeroplane safely! The golden rule is always having more fuel than you need for your trip plus a reserve. Pilots should always calculate the amount of fuel that they need for a particular flight and add enough for at least a 45-minute diversion.

Chapter Seventeen
Yet More Adventures!

'Forced Field' landing practice is an important exercise. I had a student, Dominic, and we were due to fly that part of the syllabus—in which we simulate landing in a field because of an engine failure. As with student Colin, this involved finding a suitable field in which to land: then I, the instructor, would pull the throttle to idle power, set the aircraft at best glide speed, and we would simulate landing in this field. Once we were sure that we could get into the field, we would abort the landing, throttle up and climb away (not forgetting, of course, that the law requires an aeroplane to be a minimum distance of 500 ft from any person vehicle, vessel or structure). Having demonstrated this exercise, I would let the student have a go at the same manoeuvre while helping him verbally.

On this particular day, the weather was a bit cloudy, and the forecast was that a weather front would close-in later—so we knew that conditions would get worse. So, with the weather in mind, we were considering whether to do another exercise, for example, 'Circuits' instead of 'Forced Field Landings' but a helicopter pilot flying out to the west reported to everyone on frequency that the sky was clear as far as Dorking, so we took off and headed in that direction. Well, the friendly 'eggbeater' pilot was right, and we found an open patch of sky with a nice suitable field below, suitable in size, shape and slope, with no power cables. They tend to spoil your day if you fly into them!

Anyway, while Dominic was concentrating on bringing the Shadow down, attempting to land in our selected field, I noticed that between us and Redhill Aerodrome, the sky was clouding over. We were being boxed in. The clouds were like Indians surrounding our cowboy camp. Luckily, these were not thunder clouds as I remembered from my early days, but they warranted being watched.

I kept my concerns to myself, as student Dom was concentrating hard on practising his exercise. I was watching him and the deteriorating weather, and with the clouds getting more threatening, I did start to work out a plan that might involve actually landing in the field if we became clouded-in. Dom then, too, noticed that the cloud was coming closer, so I told him not to worry but to carry on; and I told him that we could always land in the field if we had to—but I could see that he was getting concerned—me, too, but not so much from a safety point of view. We were OK there, but more from an inconvenience and logistical point of view. Once landed in this field, we would have had to leave the Shadow, go back to Redhill to get tie-downs, return to the field, discover whether there were cows anywhere in the vicinity (as they eat everything) then find the farmer, eat humble pie for having landed in his field and then, on another day, fly or drive back to the field to fly the aircraft out and back to Redhill. What a Palava that would have been!

Anyway, while Dominic was continuing to practise, I intently watched as the clouds were in a line moving south to north and we were west of them. I also noticed that while the clouds were moving quite quickly, there were occasional gaps.

These clouds were like a moving fence with the occasional panel temporarily missing. Sometimes, the gap was small, and then, a bigger gap would appear. We needed a very large gap in the clouds because we didn't want to be crossing and get trapped in a cloud—heaven forbid that the gap should close on us!

I called Redhill Air Traffic Control and asked how clear the airfield was, because if it was also clouded over, there was no point getting through *this* cloud fence and then finding bad weather beyond. If that had been the case, I had resigned myself to landing in this field, but luckily, Redhill Air Traffic Control told me that no, the weather was still good and the airfield was clear, so while Dave practised, I waited my time and watched for a suitably large gap in the cloud fence and, after many small gaps, there was at last a very large one.

I took back control of the little Shadow, throttled up full-throttle and headed straight for the gap, motoring through with the Shadow going at great speed and once through, the skies were—as Redhill had told us—clear. Panic over and back approaching Redhill, I suggested to Dom that, for the remaining time of the lesson, we join the circuit and practise landings—which we did. Unfortunately, we managed to do only one circuit before the weather front and the clouds and rain hit Redhill, so we landed and called it a day. The good thing was that we had managed to achieve what we set out to do, and it was good experience for both Dominic and for me: for him to see that a situation can change quickly and that when it does, choosing two safe options (first, to stop flying and land in a suitable field and, failing that, the second, to select a very wide gap in the cloud fence before motoring through after first making sure that the other side of the cloud bank is clear) is the wisest course of action.

Well, another happy flight with stress over and relaxation and a cup of coffee at the end.

Another day, Pilot Greg and his wife went flying in our Jabiru aircraft, but at about midday, the club received a call from Greg to say that he had suffered an engine failure and had had to land in a big field, in deepest Surrey.

Greg was an excellent pilot and later became an instructor he had landed the aircraft perfectly; after gliding down without incident and he and his wife went to apologise to the owner of the field for this unexpected use of it. Greg told the owner that he had had an emergency and had been forced to land on the property. There were no crops in the field, so nothing had been damaged.

One of our club members, John, lived close to the location, and he said that he would go over to have a look and pick up Greg and his wife. I wish he hadn't got involved, though, because the owner of the property turned out to be a Lord, and our club member did not do us any favours when he told his Lordship that the Jabiru had cost forty thousand pounds, new. Armed with that information, his Lordship—who now thought that we were loaded—then decided to expect us to pay thousands of pounds if we wanted to remove our aircraft, a demand that would not have stood up in court and one which was disgraceful in the circumstances. When I heard this, I was ready to ask for assistance from the police, for it was not by choice that Greg had had to land in the field, but of necessity, in order to save his and his wife's life. After all, he was unable to stay up there with no engine.

Well, thanks to John, our club member, I had now to explain to his Lordship that while the Jabiru had cost forty thousand pounds, it was owned by fourteen people who had each shared the cost and that unlike him, a wealthy man, we were ordinary people flying microlight aircraft and were far from being well-off. His Lordship would have been acting illegally by effectively blackmailing us for the return of our aircraft, but, as a goodwill gesture from us, he did get eight hundred pounds of the business's money donated to a charity of his choosing. Although he thought he was a saint in helping a charity, in fact, he was not such a nice person in my eyes; after all, it was our money he was happy to donate, not his, so no brownie points there, my Lord—and at one point, I did nearly phone the police to get our Jabiru back.

Along with this, the Jabiru suffered a bit of damage in transit while being trailered back to Redhill, which unfortunately can happen when aircraft are moved about on a trailer.

Another of our members had his own aircraft, a type of microlight different from the ones which we at the club flew routinely. Peter preferred to be different, though. He could have bought a share in one of our Shadows, an aircraft on which he learnt to fly, but no, he had to have a different aircraft and a different engine from the ones that we had. The engine was not as good, not an Austrian 'Rotax' but a two-stroke engine from a German manufacturer.

Peter had built this aircraft himself: he was an aircraft engineer, so it was a good 'build'. That said, not the aircraft I would have chosen to fly. My view was that it was not as easy to fly, or as safe, as the Shadow. Call me boring, but I like to do some research first and get an aircraft that has an excellent safety record that is already in use so that you can get opinions and reviews of people already flying the aircraft. That applies to the engine—even more so. There were a lot of engines out there, but once again, before I bought the engine, I would do some research and call people who had used the engine on lots of flights and,, still not content, I would then search for another similar pilot who would also recommend that engine—and a flying school review was a valuable test for a good or bad aircraft and engine. Well, forget the bad; I want the good.

Anyway, that was not Peter's philosophy. He always had to be different, and one day, he took his wife on a pleasure flight from Redhill to Lydd aerodrome. All went well until he took off from the other aerodrome Lydd, which was near the coast, to return to Redhill. Not long into the flight, the engine seized, and Peter declared a Mayday on the radio—speaking to Air Traffic Control at the Aerodrome of departure. He then proceeded to find a field for a forced landing. Well, the area had many good fields, but at the end of the one, which Peter chose, there was a drainage ditch full of water. That should not have been a problem—but it turned out to be. Now, we have another one of our little 'pilot sayings' and this is it: "Aviate, Navigate, Communicate." These are the order of priority at all times and especially when things go wrong.

Well, Peter spent more time Communicating and was not Aviating or Navigating as, while his aircraft was in descent with no engine, gliding towards his field, the control tower kept asking him where he was going to land and, rather than ignoring them, or better still, turning his radio off and concentrating on flying the plane (after all, they couldn't help him from miles away) he lost his concentration in continual chatter back and forth. The result was that he mucked up the landing! He just cleared the ditch but then stalled the aircraft from about ten feet above the ground. The aircraft dropped to Earth and crashed. Poor old Peter spent a week in the hospital and worse, his wife refused to fly with him ever again!

When he was fit again and the aircraft had been repaired, he nearly did it again. He told me that he was looking at another engine from an unheard engine maker who was extremely happy to let him be a test pilot for the unproven engine. Well, I couldn't believe it, for he was destined to make the same mistake again. Thankfully, I put him right, persuading him to buy the engine which we were using, one that had hundreds of uneventful hours to its credit—and was used by nearly everybody flying aircraft similar to ours. Thankfully, my words did not fall on deaf ears, and that was the gleaming engine he went for.

Now, to my friend Desmond, who had a miraculous escape following a much earlier experience—but in a much bigger aircraft, not in a microlight.

It was a cold, sunny day when a tall, mild-mannered man, dressed in a raincoat, came to the airfield. He spoke very softly and apologetically. He told me that he had flown before but said very little more than that. We went for a trial flight, and sure enough, Desmond could fly. There was evidently very little that I needed to teach him.

Desmond told me that he worked for the church, and I think that his soft voice explained his courteous demeanour. We became good friends and flew together quite often, even driving to the Biggin Hill Air Show to which, because of flying the customers at busy weekends, I seldom get a chance to go to.

I remember, though, while at the air show, my forehead being very sore at the end of the day and realising that I had a case of sunburn on the skin of my forehead, for I had been constantly looking at the aircraft performing in the blue sky. Notwithstanding my hurting head, that was a pleasant day, I had found out that Desmond had an interesting past.

Before Desmond had committed himself to the church, as a young man, he had joined the Royal Air Force. He told me that while he was on his RAF pilot training, he went up with an instructor to practise spinning the aircraft. They were training in a jet called a 'Vampire'—an eerie name for an aircraft—with a twin boom tail. Unfortunately, in my role as an aircraft engineer, I had acquired a bit of knowledge of this aircraft, unique in its twin boom design. I had read that it had something to watch out for, in that, if the engineers had not set up the flight controls correctly to get the rudder on each boom in perfect synchronicity with the other, the aircraft might not recover from a spin if it were to enter one—intentionally, or inadvertently.

Des told me that during his flight, the instructor had deliberately put the Vampire into a spin and then said to Desmond, "Get out of that." This is where I was 'all ears', as he then told me that when he tried to stop the spin, he instead made it worse! At that point, he heard his instructor shout frantically, "Give it to me! Give it to me!" He told me that the instructor struggled with the Vampire in vain, it was still spinning and yawing down towards the ground and the ground was getting closer and closer. Then, to Desmond's surprise, he heard the anxious command, "Eject! Eject!" He then heard, "Eject! Eject!" again and then, though frantically pulling on the ejection seat activation handle above his head nothing was happening, to his horror, he then smelt the strong smell of explosive cordite—and his instructor was gone, his seat had fired by the seat rocket, and the Perspex canopy above him had gone! With the air blasting into his face, Desmond yanked and yanked on his handle, but nothing was happening. Desmond was plummeting in a stricken jet, spinning violently towards the ground, thinking that this was the end for him.

Suddenly, Desmond heard a voice in his head telling him to pull the wire cable running down the right-hand side of his ejection seat. He tugged frantically at the cable, and there was a loud bang and an enormous upward force to his back—and off he went, out of the aircraft. I now realised where this extremely brave, religious man came from, because for him, with death staring him in the face, he believed that the voice in his head had come from God.

Desmond survived and told me that he finished his flight training and went on to fly the 'Valiant' aircraft for the RAF: but he also said that while his delayed ejection from the Vampire had been successful, he said that he decided that when he left the Royal Air Force, he would repay his debt, that debt which he believed he owed to God—hence, his ongoing years helping out in the church. After that incident, Derek had indeed got his pilot's licence, going on to fly Valiant jets for many years before retiring from the forces. Unfortunately, his instructor on that day damaged his back on ejection and sadly never flew again. I now began to understand the makeup of this gentle soft spoken, mild-mannered religious man.

Aerobatic pilot, Paul, often flew his 'Pitts Special' (a biplane) from Redhill; but Paul was only ever doing very short flights of about twenty minutes, or thirty, maximum. The reason for this was simply that Paul never liked to fly the right way up: and when you are zipping around the sky, flying inverted and doing aileron-rolls and spins, upside down does tax your body a bit. Hence, after twenty minutes, you are a bit knackered!

Paul realised that our Cessna 150 G-BTFS was an 'Aerobat'. This meant that it was not the normal Cessna, but one with extra strength, designed to do aerobatics. He wanted to teach me some aerobatics sitting side by side in my Cessna, and he did teach me.

We did barrel-rolls and aileron-rolls and some spinning; and I enjoyed it because, though BTFS was a little underpowered by the standards of later models, if you wanted to do a barrel roll after, you had made sure you had sufficient height above ground and the area was clear, you could. You would push the throttle fully forward, wind the speed up in a slight dive to one-hundred-and-twenty knots and then pull up—banking left or right as the case may be—and keep pulling until you started to see the earth come into view again and being upside down before levelling out when you saw the horizon again, then reducing the power to cruise power.

With the aileron roll similarly, you slightly lowered the nose, increased the power to about one twenty knots before you rotated the spectacle (the wheel) sharply, while watching the horizon as the Cessna put you inverted and rolled until the green stuff was down and the blue stuff was up again—in other words, the right way around.

I enjoyed my aerobatics with Paul, and one day, I practised what I had learnt on my little Irish cleaner, Maggie, who was foolish enough (joking) to fly with me when I showed her my barrel roll and my aileron roll. She was excited, although I am not sure that she knew what had just happened, but she *was* very excited.

One day, my fellow instructor Jim and I even decided to take my dog, Ben, for a gentle flight in the Cessna: no aerobatics this time, but giving him a flying experience in the twilight of his life. Well, he was sitting behind us as we taxied out to the runway. There was a nice space there, then we took off and straight away, Ben laid down, and no way could we get him to stand up and look out of the window to see the marvellous view. Ben only got back on his feet when we had landed. What a let-down (for us, but perhaps not for him)! In fact, we could have saved the petrol and landing fee and just taxied on the ground with him, as he would have seen exactly the same view. Still, we tried, and now Ben has gone. Rest in peace, Ben, we always remember you. I hope that he enjoyed it, anyway.

Chapter Eighteen
Dangling Carburettor and
Other Stories

One day, I took young Tony up for an air experience flight. He was flying the Shadow aircraft well—young people almost always pick up flying skills quickly. It was Tony's first flight, and I was introducing him to the training syllabus, starting with straight and level flight and getting him to do some turns.

We were approaching the reservoir (Bough Beach Reservoir, near Edenbridge in Kent). We were now onto trying some climbing and descending. The 'Shadow', which we were flying, was very new and had a wider body, only about a week in service out of the factory. I told Tony to increase the power and climb. As we climbed on full power, suddenly, the engine ran down, the RPM dropped, and the engine ran really rough. The vibration and roughness were so bad that I thought that a piston had come out of the side of the engine! I immediately took back control from my seat in the back, lowered the nose and throttled back to reduce the rough running; then, with the engine vibration now minimal, I started looking around for a field to land in—preferably one where I could land into wind.

We were by now on the other side of the reservoir, and I initially found a field directly below. While we were heading to the field, gliding down, I called Redhill Air Traffic and told them that I had a bad engine problem and may have to go down in a field near the reservoir. I then thought I would try pushing the throttle forward as the engine was—to my surprise—still running; so, my thinking that a piston might be protruding outside the engine was evidently wrong, because the engine would have stopped dead, had that been the case.

On the Shadow, and as I have mentioned before, the engine and propeller are behind the seats and so, out of view—so there was no chance of making a visual inspection from where I was sitting. On pushing the throttle to fully open, though

149

the engine was still running rough, I realised that it was still giving us power; but instead of getting the normal 6800 RPM, we could achieve only 5000 RPM and no more. I was still heading for my selected field, but we were still quite high, and I then realised that if I were to lift the nose and fly slow at 50 knots instead, we could keep our height and field hop from one to the next.

The normal cruise speed was 70 or 80 knots—but with a little help from thermal lift when I got it, I could maintain height. However, we now had a higher nose attitude, so Tony couldn't see so well over the instrument panel but, as I always looked out of the side windows, I was not bothered.

There was no way that I was going to fly across the reservoir—too risky—but there was another nice field on the other side, and I was sure that I could easily get there, even going the long route around. So, I avoided flying over water with a dodgy engine, flew the longer way round and, once past the reservoir, hit a little bit of gentle lift again, all without losing much height. So, I looked for yet another field on our return route to Redhill Aerodrome, effectively 'field-hopping' but safe—well, as safe as I could be for now, as the aircraft was flying at 50 knots with the nose high and still gaining or losing height gradually. All was good with airspeed well away from the stall speed of 35 knots. With gentle turns, I had that in check.

We field-hopped and were still at about 1100 feet above mean sea level when we got to South Godstone, a reporting point for Redhill Aerodrome—and the aerodrome was in view.

I had informed Redhill Air Traffic Control that we were still airborne with an engine problem, so they knew the score, and they told me to come straight in as, in an emergency, the airfield for that short period was all mine.

I noticed another good field below en route, after South Godstone Station, to keep in mind for a possible landing in case things did go wrong before I were to reach the aerodrome. But we were still up there, flying, and I now had the M23 motorway to cross with Redhill Aerodrome Runway 26 in full view.

The engine had kept going, albeit not smoothly, my plan now was not to do a normal approach in case my luck ran out just at the last minute if the engine gave up, so instead, I would keep as much height as I could until I was close to the runway—in other words, come in high, and when I was sure that we were going to make it, switch off both ignitions and glide in to land halfway along the runway. I did not have to worry about flap speeds or putting any flaps down as the Shadow, unlike the CT that we now fly, landed perfectly well without the use of flaps, so I stuck to my plan and switched the switches off. The engine stopped, and I gently side-slipped the Shadow until the wheels touched down.

Once on the ground, of course, we were blocking the runway, so I told Tony to stay put in the front cockpit and hauled myself through the rear crash bars and jumped out. As soon as I looked at the engine, I could see the problem straightaway, the rearmost one of the two carburettors was adrift and hanging off, restrained only by its own fuel pipe, throttle cable and choke cable. The carburettors are held on to the little 'Rotax' engine by special rubber sockets connected to the two inlet manifolds. There is a jubilee-type clip at each end of the moulded rubber socket. To get the engine started again and then taxi back to the hangar, I took the clip off the end of the socket where the carburettor had detached, and then I pushed the carburettor back on temporarily, putting the clip in my pocket as I had no tools.

I switched on the ignition switches, pulled the starter cord, and off she fired. This time, the engine sounded as it should, luckily, no worse for the incident, sweet, with no vibration. I thought it best not to say anything to Tony after we got back, this happening on his first air experience flight; but sadly, nevertheless, that was the last I saw of him.

This was a brand-new aircraft, and after examination, it took a moment to find the cause of the problem. I discovered that the rubber socket for the carburettor had a manufacturing fault, in that it had a moulding blowhole void which would fill with two-stroke oil that was injected into the manifold. The result was like putting soap onto a tight wedding ring to get it off: the oil would make the carburettor fall off with the vibration every time it occurred.

After replacing that rubber socket and checking the other one, the engineer in me thought it safer to replace the two single air-filters with one dual air filter, so that each carburettor holds its brother in place and the vibration is reduced: 'belt and braces' as we call it in the trade.

I did realise after the event though, that I was lucky that the throttle and choke cable had held the carburettor while it was waggling around in the wind—and also lucky that the rubber fuel pipe had restrained the carburettor from hitting the propeller. Had it been the carburettor closest to the propellor that had disconnected, we would definitely have been in the field with worse vibration—from a shattered propellor!

It was impressive that with only one cylinder of the two working, the engine could still produce 5000 RPM.

The wide-body Shadow, a good little glider with the Rotax 582 64 horsepower engine, a good little dual-ignition two-stroke engine.

Stan became a good pilot. He worked in the heart of London by night and became a private pilot in his leisure time. We trained him and, being a very good pilot, he picked up the art of decision-making when things go wrong—a quality with which not all pilots are blessed, even though one of the most important objectives of pilot training is to acquire the skill of 'captaincy', to be the pilot-in-command of a passenger-carrying aeroplane and so, to take all decisions that need to be taken.

An, as a solo pilot, was flying one of our Shadow aircrafts and was seated in the front with the back seat empty. Stan decided to practise a forced landing in a field, simulating the situation where the engine has unexpectedly stopped. To practise this, he didn't shut down the engine (one doesn't, when practising, in case the engine won't restart when needed) but instead, throttled the engine back to idle, simulating a failure—and started his glide.

Well, he picked from a distance what looked like a suitable field but, when he got closer, the field was far from good, with low power cables supported by telegraph poles straight across it. Also, it sloped upwards, had houses on the left-hand side, trees at the end and trees on the right-hand side. If that was not enough, there was a horse trough in the middle of the field, too.

As Stan got closer to his chosen field, he realised that his choice of a practice field had not been ideal (it was bad, actually, failing the size, shape slope, surface and surroundings assessment which is drummed into pilots during the training exercise); and from very close to it, he decided to abort his approach and landing, open the throttle and climb away to find another field. To Stan's horror, as he pushed the throttle fully forward to its stop, the throttle-cable snapped, and the engine ran back to idle! Like it or not, Stan was now with no other option than to land in this grotty field, whether he liked it or not; and, he hoped, stay in one piece and, if possible, keep the aircraft in one piece too.

Well, after he landed, he called us to tell us all about it. We hitched up the Shadow's trailer and drove to his landing site. There he was, uninjured, and I was amazed to see the pilot happy and the aircraft undamaged—not a mean feat. I had expected to see the aircraft with at least a broken nose leg as it was not a smooth field. Stan, the magician of the day, had missed the horse trough, flown under the power cables and landed upslope without breaking anything!

My friend asked if we were going to fly the aircraft out. I decided not, as we needed an easterly wind and that does not happen much, never mind the other shortcomings of the field. I imagined the headlines in the next day's newspaper: "Student pilot lands aircraft in unsuitable field successfully but chief flying instructor kills himself after taking off downhill with wind behind him, and then flying under power cables." That would have been a disastrous scoop, so I instead took the safe option, took the aircraft apart and returned to Redhill by trailer with it in tow on the road.

One day, we took an air experience booking for a one-hour flight from a young 17-year-old called Mary. Mary was a pretty girl with, it seemed, a dark cloud hanging over her. We sat her in the front of the Shadow and strapped her in. I clambered into the back seat to sit behind young Mary.

We lined up on runway 26L, I opened the throttle, and the aircraft started to roll and gain speed along the ground. I applied some rudder to keep the aircraft in the middle of the runway, the nose lifted at around 45 knots, and I left the nose just above the ground as the aircraft accelerated to flying speed. Mary got very excited at the sensation in the climb, and I told her to 'follow me through' on the controls (that is, feel how the controls moved as I moved them), and up we went.

When we reached an altitude of 1200 feet, I levelled the aircraft, throttled back to cruise power and then asked Mary to move the stick forward, then back, nose down, nose up then to bank and turn the Shadow left and right. she was a fast learner, like most young people. She was a natural, turning left, turning right, climbing and descending the little Shadow.

When the flight came to an end, I asked Mary how she felt. She was pulsing with excitement! We joined the others for a coffee where I told her that she was a natural, that most youngsters pick up flying quickly; and I asked her if she was going to train for her pilot's licence. It was a sad day for all of us. Mary told me that she was terminally ill and had only a year to 18 months to live: and with that bombshell, she took out a small notebook from her pocket and showed us a 'bucket list' of things that she had always wanted to do. There was flying in a microlight, water skiing, flying in a Tiger Moth, a trip in a balloon, on a boat, horse-riding and even scuba diving.

I desperately tried to persuade her to learn to fly or even just join the flying club, but she chose not to. I did manage to get her to our club barbecue that weekend where we plied her with food and drink. We asked Mary to keep in touch, but she never did: and months later, we were all devastated to hear that young Mary had completed her bucket list and had then taken her own life. How sad. Events such as this always make one realise that life is indeed short and so unpredictable.

A very sad episode for all of us in the school.

On a lighter note, next door to me lived my neighbour Samuel. The house which my family and I lived in was semi-detached, and occasionally, in the early days before I started the flying school, I would take my Shadow home in the trailer and work on the fuselage and engine—wings off, of course—in the comfort of my garage.

It was a nice day, and I had just refitted the engine with its pusher propellor and moved the aircraft, minus its wings, which I left in the trailer. I choked the wheels, made sure all areas were clear, primed the fuel system (by squeezing the fuel supply rubber bulb several times) then pushed the choke lever to the rich position, flicked on the single ignition switch and pulled the starter cord.

The little Rotax 447 single ignition engine sprang into life, and I moved the throttle lever off 'idle'. The engine accelerated, I watched the gauges to check their operation, and all was good, everything was functional.

When I looked through the arc of the whirling propellor though, to my horror, I noticed that the air-wash from pusher propeller had decapitated all the heads of my neighbour, Samuel's flowers in his front garden, and he loved his garden. There were only stems left with the heads of the flowers mostly on the Lawn! *Oh, hell*, I thought. I quickly switched off the engine and frantically looked to see if my neighbour was outside and had noticed and if I was about to get the rollicking of my life. Luckily, he did not appear so, and I am not proud of this, but it is funny (I was young then) I got down on all fours and crept below Samuel's front bay window, collected every rose and tulip-head and put them in a dustbin bag. Of course, there was no chance of sticking the heads back on! Samuel's garden did look peculiar, with plants with stems but no flowers.

I quickly put the Shadow's fuselage back in the trailer and waited to see if Samuel appeared. Had he done so, I would have owned up—but he did not appear, so I didn't tell him, and luckily, whether or not he didn't notice, I will never know but nothing was said. I am still hoping to go to heaven as after all it was unintentional, "Honest, Your Honour."

Another day, while relaxed in our porta cabin, I had a frantic phone call from a gentleman I didn't recognise. He sounded agitated, so much so that I wondered what the hell we might have done. After getting deep into the call, Douglas told us that he was in Wales and had been out for a local flight climbing out in his Shadow when he was rapidly approached by a very low flying Royal Airforce Tornado jet aircraft which was on a collision course with him.

Douglas had a young man's voice, broad Welsh, but when you met him, he was one of those people who was nothing like one might have thought from his voice: in fact, he was much older than his voice implied. He told me that he had been so close to the Tornado flying up the valley, that he could see the whites of the pilot's eyes. He also saw the panic on the face of the RAF Pilot as he manoeuvred his Tornado to avoid the little Shadow.

The Tornado pilot had engaged 'reheat' to avoid Douglas—which didn't help Douglas as the thrust from the Tornado's jet pipes as they lit up, blew the Shadow downwards, lifting Dug off his seat and the engine upwards off its mountings. Douglas had hit his head on the canopy which broke, and he was knocked unconscious.

The RAF pilot called back to base to sadly announce that he had killed the microlight pilot! Meanwhile, Douglas had come round and found the little Shadow still flying. Unbeknownst to Douglas at that time, the propellor had hit the underside of the centre section as the force had lifted the engine on its mountings. The front canopy had been shattered and the jet blast had blown a hole of about eighteen inches in the wing leading edge—yet, the little Shadow was still flying.

Douglas flew back to his home where he had his own field in which to land. The CAA later criticised him for flying the damaged Shadow on for thirty minutes following the incident, instead of landing straight away; but Dug pointed out that he was flying in the Welsh valleys with no airfields and nowhere else to land.

What an amazing story he told, but the frantic call to me was one of desperation. The Shadow factory had repaired the little Shadow—all paid for by the Ministry of Defence—and Douglas had flown the repaired aircraft: but he was unhappy, as it kept turning right. His main concern was that the factory had not replaced the wings, which Douglas feared had been over-stressed by the severe negative gravitational force to which he and the Shadow had been subjected in the incident. Both he and the aircraft had been pushed downwards by the jet efflux from the Tornado, especially when 'reheat' (extra jet power) had been selected by the Tornado's pilot in an effort to get out of the way!

I did agree with Douglas that after such an incident, where he evidently pulled a great amount of negative 'g' possibly over stressing them, I would have also felt better throwing those damaged wings away and flying with new ones was the thing to do. So, Douglas had arguments with the Shadow factory as they stubbornly didn't think changing the wings was necessary and had lost confidence in it. Douglas was so upset that in that first phone call, he authorised us to get the police involved if, when we went to the factory to pick up his Shadow, we were refused permission to collect it. Fortunately, it did not come to that. I suggested a plan to the factory: the factory would supply a wing kit; we at the club would create and fit a new set of wings to Douglas little Shadow, and we would test fly it.

I suggested that we would work with the support of the factory as its agent in this case, because there was no way Dug would now let the Shadow factory anywhere near his aircraft ever again. So that was the plan, and all parties were happy. We got an urgent delivery of a wing kit and rebuilt the aircraft, test flew it—and it flew straight and level. Douglas was as pleased as Punch, so much so that he advertised our business, and he told everyone of his joy at returning to the sky again knowing that he had a new set of unstressed wings holding him up and that the aircraft flew properly—and straight!

The only slightly downside was that from then on, we had to travel all the way to Wales every year to carry out the Permit to Fly inspection (which is like a vehicle's MoT) and to check-fly the aircraft: but that was all part of the service.

Another day in the early years when I was a pilot not an instructor, I had invited Frank from the control tower to fly with me in the Shadow, and we took to the air. Now, when the Shadow first got its Permit to Fly, it was weight-limited to no more than one hundred and fifty kilograms, empty. To achieve that, everything had to be as light as possible and that meant that—apart from a light, weaker undercarriage—we also had to put up with the underpowered 38 hp Rotax 447 engine. That was a good engine, but it was a two-stroke and so, was high-revving. At that time, engine manufacturers had not developed engines with a dual-ignition system (i.e., two ignition systems) so the engine had only one sparkplug and was very light to help the aircraft keep to its specified maximum allowable weight. Because of this, the engine failures that I experienced were all on two-strokes and most—though not all—were because of ignition problems.

In particular, there was a little roller bearing at the 'small end' working hard where the piston is connected to the 'connecting rod', which failed on many microlights. Luckily for me, the manufacturers brought out a free-rolling, thirty-one-needle bearing as a direct replacement. Before that, the old bearing was the cause of one of my failures but what I am getting at is, that these engine failures in those early days on that little four-four-seven 38-horsepower engine certainly taught me a few things about flying!

We were always taught to plan for the unexpected engine failure by 'field-hopping' and going around the reservoir instead of directly over it, for example. Anyway, my flight with Frank was enjoyable. We flew over the Surrey and Kent countryside. He was flying the Shadow sitting in the front tandem seat, and I, in my normal position as an instructor in the rear seat. We had flown for around an hour, before—and you have probably guessed it—that little four-four-seven then decided to run rough on one cylinder. The loss of power meant that we were not keeping our height and so, we searched for a field to land in.

Now I throttled back to idle, set the aircraft at its best glide speed and noticed what looked like a good field ahead of us: and what looked like a good field to the right of us. I didn't switch the ignition off because at idle power the engine was smoother; and because it was running, it helped to extend the glide slightly—but it did nothing else for us.

We were still some ways away from both fields. Luckily, there was very little wind. I had to make a choice—which field was I to go for? But at this stage, I wasn't close enough to either field to see what the ground was like. Was it flat, did it have power cables, what was the surface like? Those questions would be answered as we got closer.

I decided to turn the aircraft right and to pick the field on my right: it looked slightly bigger from this distance. As Frank and I got closer he, being in front of me had the better view. We noticed that the field which we were going for had cows in its top left corner: also, we now noticed that the field was not flat but had a downhill slope from our approach direction and, as we were on final approach, landing speed set, I found that I could not see down the hill! (A flat field or if not, an uphill slope is always to be preferred to a downhill slope when landing: once on the ground, as the aircraft slows and stops more quickly).

We then flew over the preceding field (these fields being part of a farm) and in one field, I noticed that there were lots of strawberry pickers: but I also noticed that not one picker stopped picking the fruit or looked at us, as we flew over. *How odd,* I thought. *Maybe they have seen an aircraft land in the field before?* The cows were stationary in the corner of the field to our left, but because I still could not see the bottom end of the field, I had to suspect that there may be cows there too. I decided, therefore, not wanting to hit a cow—better to land early where I could see open space in the centre of the field rather than land further in—but in order to do that, I had to bring the Shadow down slightly hard and fast. This as I expected splayed the little, weak, Shadow's undercarriage.

Luckily, there were no more cows, so Frank, I and the cows lived to fight another day, the aircraft with minor damage. Amazingly, as we walked up to the other field on the way to apologise to the farmer, we ran into the strawberry pickers, but on the dirt road, before we got to them, there was the lovely waft of strawberries, and I noticed that a whole box had been spilt from the tractor-trailer, and the wheels of the tractor had mashed the fruit into the ground resulting in a beautiful aroma. I apologised to the strawberry pickers for choosing their field. "Ah, yes," one said, "we did think you sounded a bit rough as you flew over us."

When we arrived at the farm shop and spoke to the owner, we found that he hadn't realised that we had even had a problem—but that did not stop his moaning, telling us that we were the second aircraft to land on his property. The first, he complained, was a Hurricane during wartime that had crashed, burying itself in the ground but still to be found. Thankfully, the pilot had descended by parachute safely—so that was a blessing. I did think later, though, how ungrateful the owner was to the Hurricane and its pilot for fighting and risking his life for King and Country. People are very strange, aren't they?

Anyway, we got a taxi back to Redhill, picked up the trailer, and once again, it was becoming a habit, dismantled and collected the little Shadow before the cows could eat it. How pleased I was in later years that the CAA permitted the increase of microlight weight so that we could fit the heavier Rotax 503 fifty horse-power-dual-ignition engine on our little Shadow.

Chapter Nineteen
The Last Days of Shadow Manufacture and Various Repairs

The Shadow factory had gone into liquidation. We had tried to help it stay afloat. The manufacturer had asked us all for one thousand pounds to invest in the company, but unfortunately, that was not enough to save it and eventually, it stopped trading. Later, though, someone bought the little Shadow factory, and the manufacturer became known as 'Shadow Aircraft Company'.

The original Shadows had always been snug in the cockpit, to say the least: pilot (and passengers) were sitting in a narrow 'Fibrelam' bathtub. It was safe Fibrelam, a brilliant composite-fibre type of material with a sandwich of 'honeycomb' which gave it the strength of steel and the ability to absorb shocks and vibration. Before I used it in the building of the Shadow kits, I had seen its use in floorboards, in the cabins of commercial aircraft, when I worked for British Airways.

That said, it wasn't cheap stuff. The designer of the Shadow—a brilliant designer who made this little safe aircraft—experimented at one time, using an aluminium honeycomb instead of Fibrelam to save cost, but scrapped the idea when he found that he was often retightening the undercarriage bolts because the aluminium was crushing, whereas the Fibrelam had a 'memory' and would crush but spring back to its original state.

One of the small mistakes that he made was not one of safety but one of cockpit size. He was a man of slight build, and although he added three inches more than his width to the width of the Shadow bathtub to allow for wider pilots, it was still snug. I was slim too, in the early days, but even I seemed to struggle on occasions with twisted seatbelts jammed each side between me and the Fibrelam side of the bathtub. When owners and schools suggested to the designer that it would be nice to make a wider cockpit, that was said to be impossible to change from the original design, unfortunately, because of the cost of recertification by the CAA.

A company in South Africa which had a licence to make and sell Shadows on behalf of the UK company did, though, redesign the cockpit of the Shadow—increasing width and height—and was able to get the certification done through the South African authorities; but there had to be many other changes made, too. The benefit of that was that once it had been done in South Africa, it was straightforward to mirror the legislation in the UK.

Good old CAA! I can remember hearing that the designer had said that it was harder and very expensive to get even the new elevator trim system certified in this country than it was to get the whole aircraft changed and certified in South Africa.

The new Shadow Aircraft Company never ever made the original smaller version of the Shadow. Instead, all the new ones were wider and were known as the D-D Shadow Wide-Body. It also had the bigger 64-horsepower Rotax 582 engine. No more seat belt problems and room to spare! Unfortunately, the wide-body Shadow came too late for me to fly with a young lady pilot who wanted to try the Shadow. She arrived on her motorbike but sadly could not get her bottom fully down onto the seat in the front cockpit. She said that she could manage by sitting 'on the slant' with her bottom lifted for a short while, but I didn't think that that was safe, so we didn't fly. Sorry Susan!

The new Shadow Aircraft Company was clever, though. The company asked me if I would be interested in borrowing their new factory aircraft for a month to use at my school. Well! What a machine! Bigger cockpit and bigger Rotax 582 engine—much faster, with the same safe flying characteristics as the earlier models. That sales ploy did the trick as, after using it in the school, we didn't want to return it: we just had to get one and we did, G-ZY.

Because I am an aircraft engineer by profession, and at the time, we were operating four Shadows, I got to know the little aircraft and engines well—as did the pilots who flew them. I received a desperate telephone call from Charles, who complained that he had bought a Shadow but could not get it to take off. He had not ever managed to get it airborne. He had tried the take-off run many times but failed to reach take-off speed and lift off.

When he bought the aircraft to me, a quick inspection showed what the problem was—or should I say, what the problems were. The aircraft had had many illegal extras fitted. There was a little 'SU' electric fuel pump, extra to the normal engine operated pump: these electric pumps, normally fitted on the British Leyland 'Mini' or on the old 'Morris 1000' cars are not designed to be used on aircraft. There was also a huge, heavy, so-called (for want of a better description) 'flux capacitor' nothing like to flux capacitor on the DeLorean in the film Back to The Future this one fixed in the rear cockpit to work the compass which was in the front. This looked as though it had come from a World War Two Bomber.

There were lots of extras that were not supposed to be there; and, along with these, the main problem was that someone had replaced the brake cables which run from the pedals in the cockpit to the brake shoes on the wheels—but seemingly (I think) the cables were lorry cables. It must have been a 'Murphy' who had fitted these cables, them having square ends that had to fit into a circular hole in the brake lever the epitome of Murphys Law. Whoever did it must have had to force the square cable end into the round hole, jamming it with the result that there was no chance of the cable end rotating—so that the brakes were on all the time! Naturally, when Charles had attempted to take-off, with all the extra weight from his illegal accessories and the seized brakes, he had no chance of getting this little Shadow airborne!

I presented Charles with his surplus spares in a big cardboard box marked 'Surplus to requirements'.

We were moved to the other side of the airfield from the east gate, with our aircraft hangared in Hangar Two. One late afternoon, Arthur and I had moved the Shadows over to the hangar at the end of the flying day. The 'Jabiru' was still parked outside the club office, and I had asked Jeremy to bring the Jabiru over from the club to the hangar. Well, Arthur and I waited and waited: and time was ticking on and on.

Eventually, we had waited long enough so decided to walk back to the club to investigate the delay. Another lump-in-the-throat moment! As we turned the corner to get to the club, we saw our Jabiru, nose leg smashed up. It had run away, gone down an incline—and crashed into a concrete block and a fence outside the helicopter hangar.

Jeremy had lost control, but there was one bonus, if I can call it that: while the aircraft was running away, Jeremy did do one good thing: he switched the ignition off, stopping it and saving the engine and propellor before the nose leg hit the obstacle. Along with the nose wheel, the main undercarriage had run over the concrete block so that needed to be replaced too and what a pain it was trying to get a broken aircraft back into Hangar 2. We never let Jeremy taxi an aircraft alone ever again, and sadly, he was not up to getting his pilot's licence.

I started teaching Anthony in the CT, and he was progressing well. He was taking in all the information that I was giving him. When learning to fly, the more flying that one does, the quicker one is able to get one's licence; and because Anthony was almost retired, he flew with me about three of four times each week.

One day, my friend and student at the time, Anthony, asked if we could fly from Redhill to Goodwood, land, have a cup of tea, then fly to Shoreham Aerodrome and follow the coast towards Lydd, stop; and then return to Redhill. You can see that he was getting a lot of experience from his flying sorties. Anthony got to solo, and the other students remarked, "Is he solo already?"

"Yes," I said. "Well, he flies at least three times a week!"

I repeated to them, "The more flying you do, the quicker you'll get your licence."

The CT is certainly not as easy to fly as the Cessna when practising landing without flaps. In the Cessna, it seems like a non-event: but in the Flight Design CT, the approach with landing flap is steep. If a flap failure occurs, to achieve the correct landing speed, you have to keep the nose high. Unfortunately, when doing this, you come in lower, and you can't see very well over the instrument panel because it is higher than it would normally be.

Well, as luck would have it, on one of my last dual-training flights with Anthony when we flew to Headcorn Airfield, as Anthony selected landing flap the bloody things seemed to hesitate, then to deploy. We did a 'go around' at Headcorn, and the same thing happened again when we selected flaps—nothing! We selected again and then—down they went.

When we got back to Redhill, I traced the problem to the circuit board behind the CT's bulkhead—a fault that I have experienced since—but, apart from changing the board, so that was yet another repair satisfactorily completed. (I had to give Anthony a lot of practice at flapless landings, now more than usual, as he was by then in the solo phase of his training and I knew that flaps not working could happen again without me sitting next to him. Anthony, in fact, got his Microlight Licence, and then, he bought an aeroplane and obtained his Instrument Rating, then learnt to fly helicopters; so, Anthony has all three licences now. His aircraft has an autopilot and all the gadgets—marvellous! Well done, Anthony, a nice guy and also an expert on flapless CT landings)!

Chapter Twenty
The Dream Continues

In my thirty six years of flying, there have been many times when an aircraft appeared into view suddenly. That tends to be how one first sees other aircraft when flying, despite keeping a good 'lookout'. Of course, we have always changed course to avoid the risk of an airborne collision, but luckily, to my knowledge, over those thirty six years, there have been only two very close near-misses that I can think of.

The first was in the early days of training, in the Shadow, when I was doing circuits with my student who sat in the front seat of the Shadow with me sitting in the back seat. Everything was going well. We were taking off for the fifth time, 'flying the square' round the airfield, then landing—and immediately throttling up and taking off again.

This time, we had again taken off, turned right for our 'crosswind leg' and then right again for our downwind leg of the circuit. I reported to Redhill Tower that I was 'downwind', and the tower told me to report 'finals'. That told me that there were no aircraft in front of me and that I was 'Number One'.

I then instructed the student to turn right again, onto the last leg of the circuit—that being the 'base leg' before 'finals to land'. It was by luck that just before we were about to turn onto finals, we heard another aircraft on frequency, announcing to the Air Traffic Control that *he* was now on finals.

Hell! I thought. We were about to turn finals. The student had the better view ahead, being in the front of the Shadow, so over the intercom, I asked James, "Is the aircraft just landing, is it ahead of us?"

"I can't see it," James replied.

I frantically looked for this aircraft from my back seat. My seat in the rear was under the wings, limiting my view, so I asked James anxiously, "Is he on your left, then?"

"No, I can't see him," said James. We had to find this bloody aircraft and quickly. Then, almost as soon as his breath had come out, James shouted, "There he is!" I looked frantically for the other aircraft's position, and to my horror, he was not far from our left wingtip. I immediately took control and pushed the control column forward and right aggressively. As our aircraft started its spiral descent to the right, I remember doing mentally a damage control assessment; and thinking *OK, if the aircraft takes-off our left wingtip we should still be OK*— of course, forgetting that on the left wing towards the tip was the left aileron, and that was my method of controlling the aircraft in the roll axis!

Anyway, after we had moved, I counted, "One, Two, Three," in my head. My left wing was high in the sky, and my right wing pointing at the ground. As soon as I had reached the count of three, there was a loud 'Whoosh', and this PA28 (a much bigger four seat low wing 'Piper' aircraft) flew straight over our left wingtip and appeared right in front of us, then below us, on finals for Runway 26. I waited for a few seconds to see if the PA28 pilot called the tower to report that he had just been involved with a near-miss, but there was a stunned silence. The other aircraft had not even seen us, and of course, we were, until the last moment, at exactly the same height.

I reported the near-miss to the air traffic controller who, for a few seconds, did not reply. I suspect that he was a little stunned, too! My student was spooked, and it took me some time to get him back to flying the aeroplane in that lesson, but when I told him that it was all over and to concentrate on flying the aircraft again, I gave him back control but helped him with this landing: in fact, I think that *I* did the landing.

Although the student had suggested straight after the near-miss that we land, I pointed out to him that it was important to forget what had just happened and to continue. We did a touch-and-go and took off again, doing another three circuits before finishing for a cup of tea and reflecting on our experience the student went on to be an instructor so carrying on was the right course of action. I think best not to dwell on such an event but to get back flying straight away— a little bit like the film 'Top Gun' filmed in later years when, after Tom Cruise's 'flat spin' and his reluctance to fly again, his Commanding Officer tells the instructors to 'Get him up again'.

One of the biggest risks in our incident (and any similar incident) was that after the near-miss, for a few seconds, we were stunned—that is, momentarily shocked into inaction, the pilot in a dream—and, of course, that's a risk because it's no good surviving a near-miss then hitting the ground as you remain stunned and can't snap out of it.

My second, near-miss was recently, within the last eighteen months. Pilot Jeremy and I decided to do a nice cross-country flight from Redhill Aerodrome to Lydd Airfield, which is on the Kent coast. We got there with no problems, paid our landing fee, and went for refreshments. We returned to our Flight Design CTSW and taxied out from the 'apron' (that part of the airfield where aircraft may be parked) and started to enter Runway 21. As I was lining up, with Jeremy in control of the aircraft, I pressed the transmit button, which is on the top of the control column, calling the tower to ask whether they wanted me to do a non-standard right turn to depart to the north after take-off. "Yes, please," was the reply.

We were then given clearance to take-off. Jeremy was flying, and he opened the throttle to full power, and the CT started to accelerate along this vast runway. We lifted off about a third of the way along, and when crossing the far end of the runway we turned right as ordered, while remaining in the climb.

We were still in the climb at fifteen hundred feet when we heard another aircraft call Lydd Tower to say that he was about to join the 'overhead' for Lydd. (Joining overhead the field—and at 1500 ft—is the standard procedure when approaching that airfield).

The tower replied to him and then, just after the air traffic controller called us and asked what height we were at and before I could answer, I saw a 'Kantana' that I recognised, out of Redhill about two seconds from hitting us. He caught Jeremy by surprise but as I saw it first, I said, "Give it to me!"

Once again, I turned the aircraft aggressively to the right while pitching down, and the Katana went past us on the left side. I was then able to reply to the Lydd air traffic controller, telling him, "Yes, we were at 1500 ft and had just passed the Katana." That was evidently why the controller had called us—he suspected a problem, and his fears were realised.

Phew! Dangerous this flying, LOL!

On the few occasions of flying with Anthony in his Robin 'DR 400', apart from autopilot, there are other electronic systems, screens and gizmos. On his map screen, a device call ADSB (Automatic Dependent Surveillance Broadcast) shows his aircraft and other aeroplanes in the area. If one gets close, a visual warning is shown on the screen—perfect. There is now a bit of kit that we can swap from aircraft to aircraft, which tunes into a navigational aid called

'Skydemon', which can be displayed on a mobile phone or pad which gives similar warning of other traffic within the range set on the equipment—although you will never beat a good look out! (Some say that these gizmos are detrimental to look out because they require eyes inside the cockpit to look at them instead of looking outside).

It was a nice sunny day and Mark, one of our instructors, had been doing an air experience flight in one of our Wide-Body Shadows. He was just about to land on Runway Three Six.

The airfield had been out of action for a while as there had been contractors digging up parts of the airfield, putting wide water drainage pipes alongside the runways. The runways were untouched, but pilots needed to be careful not to go over the soft areas where a trench had been dug, a pipe laid and the earth replaced, as it needed to settle and harden.

It always amazes me that some pilots—and I'm afraid that that included Mark in this instance—are too eager to exit the runway as fast as they can, even if it is not safe to do so. Remember Steven? After landing in forty-knot winds, he was so eager to vacate the runway having been told to do so by Air Traffic Control, that the wind tipped him onto his wingtip, turning the aircraft upside down. Now Mark, though he knew that he would get stuck if he didn't avoid the soft repaired ground, still proceeded to go on to it, get himself stuck in it; and then, rather than tell Air Traffic Control that his aircraft was stuck, I am afraid, was determined to rev hell out of the engine, determined to get the aircraft unstuck.

Now, the correct thing to do is to try gently to accelerate the engine, to provide more thrust to the propellor and see if that does the job. If this doesn't do the trick, going to full power is very likely to dig the nose gear in more and inevitably snap it off. The *best* thing to do is for you and your passenger to get out and, with the aircraft being lighter, push it off the soft ground.

Mark, though, eager to not upset the air traffic controller, sacrificed the Shadow aircraft and revved up so much that he not only snapped off the nose gear tube but also bent the main landing gear and when that happened, the propellor touched the ground, the blades snapped; and the tail also leaned over and bent on the tail skid!

To cut a long story short, rather than shut down and alight the aircraft, push and if that failed ask for help (after all, he had the radio) we were now into a broken propeller, bent fin, broken nose leg and a bent main undercarriage. Well done, Mark! You can guess that, as he was an instructor, I was not impressed with a bad choice, broken aircraft out of service and with the expense and labour involved in repair.

One of the lucky things was that because we could do the repairs ourselves, we did save on the cost of labour but nevertheless, the less damaged an aircraft is, the better, as the routine servicing and wear and tear defects were enough to contend with. We had a spare engine for each type of Shadow, which is a spare engine for the wide-body Shadow and a spare engine for the smaller CD Shadow aircraft: and the advantage of having the spare power plants was that the fleet was never grounded as, whenever we needed to 'decoke' (clean out carbon deposits) from one engine, we would simply fit 'one we made earlier'.

Friend and retired high-ranking commercial pilot came to fly with me. Jim, though now retired, during his career as the chief pilot of a major airline, Jim had bought a Shadow, and he had a nice 'Lynton' Trailer in which to house it; and whenever I went over to Jim's to maintain his aircraft, his wife always made us a lovely cup of tea and got the cake and biscuits out. They were lovely people.

It is always difficult when you are teaching someone who has more qualifications than you do but, of course, going from flying a huge MacDonald Douglas DC10 to a small Shadow microlight was a drastic change for Jim. My friend, young Matt, now also a commercial pilot, once told me about his friend, a British Airways pilot who normally flew the 747 'Jumbo' jet. Matt told me that when he let his friend have a go at landing the CT, he would almost certainly attempt to land the aircraft from about the height of a double-decker bus, thinking he was still sitting high up in the cockpit of his jumbo.

Jim, though, did not like anybody telling him what to do. After all, as chief pilot for a major airline, he had been used to giving orders, rather less so taking them; and a couple of times, when we were practising landing the little Shadow, or doing circuits, Jim would tell me that he was going to try something, and when I said that we needed permission from air traffic control, he would ignore me— and, of course, the tower (that is, the air traffic controller on duty in the control tower) would then sarcastically ask whether we had a problem, which was a polite way of asking us what the hell we were doing! I would have to explain and would say to Jim, "There you are, Jim, I warned you!" After all that said, Jim, of course, was an excellent pilot and a valued member of our flying club.

One thing Jim used to talk about often was 'the men' in the 'Glass House', those men to whom he referred being the Civil Aviation Authority. Jim, I suspect, had had some run-ins with them during his career with that major airline as well. Well, luckily for me at this time, I had not had any contact or problems with the authority. Unfortunately, in later years, that was it destined to change. I would find out that along with the nice clever guys therein, there were also some rather less so.

Now, leaving the less-nice and less-clever ones aside for one minute, there was a nice examiner, Mr Tanner, a CAA surveyor, who conducted the oral examination for our engineer's Type Licence on the Boeing aircraft, the 707 and 737, during the early 1980s. Mr Tanner wasn't a 'pushover'. If you did not know the ins and outs of that aircraft, you would definitely be found out. You had to have done your studying on the Boeing 707 but, that said, if you had been successful—though he was not allowed to tell you the result of your oral test before it was official—he would ask you what you were up to at the weekend; and, after you had told him, if you had passed, he would tell you to have a good weekend.

Years later, when I went for my Boeing 737 Type Licence, I was studying so hard my nose kept bleeding. As a teenager, there were times when—if I did as much as touch my nose—off it would go. On top of that, if I had a slight cold a sneeze would start it for certain. The doctor had told me that it was a relief-valve to relieve pressure. After my oral test with Mr Tanner, I was in fact, off to see the specialist at the hospital to get my damned nose cauterised.

I sat in front of Mr Tanner, tissues ready in my pocket, but I knew that if my nose started bleeding during my oral test, that test would have to be stopped, and I didn't want to warn Mr Tanner about it in case he thought I was offering a feeble excuse. Well, it was really difficult not to move my head quickly or sneeze, but when the test was completed, Mr Tanner asked me what plans I had afterwards: so, I came clean and told him of my problem and that I was off to get my bloody nose cauterised at the hospital straight after leaving the CAA. He told me that I ought to have told him and he would have 'given me a break' but luckily, his kind offer wasn't needed: my nose behaved itself and I got my Boeing 737 Type Licence.

Back to the Flying

It was a lovely summer's day late in the afternoon. The wind was dead calm with infinite visibility (so to speak). I was teaching a student, Terry—long now, an experienced pilot, but this was years and years ago. We were halfway through our one-hour lesson when I looked towards the coast, about fifty miles from where we were, and noticed a thunder cloud forming. Because it was so far away, it didn't worry me. We carried on with our flight and I, with the training.

Later, when we were just passing the southern boundary of Biggin Hill Aerodrome on our return journey to Redhill, the calm flying conditions suddenly changed, and we were getting bumped around, when I looked around, I noticed that new thunderclouds were surrounding our little 'Shadow' like Indians around a Waggon Train. Biggin Hill Aerodrome was very close, so after I called up Biggin Air Traffic. I told Terry to head towards Biggin, as we were going to take the safe option and land to sit out the thunder there.

We landed, and Air Traffic Control was very nice to us. We weren't the only ones to land at Biggin for safety reasons at that time—a Cessna from Redhill also landed at Biggin, having also been caught by the sudden change in the weather.

For those potential aviators reading this, for reference, if you are flying keep well away from thunder clouds (properly called Cumulonimbus, or 'Cb' for short)! Think of them as giant vacuum cleaners sucking up air from all around. The updraught in a Cb is phenomenal, and they can move in any direction including against the wind—but one good thing, if anything, about them is that they are normally short-lived.

Having landed at Biggin, while on the ground, Terry and I hung on to the wings of our Shadow for dear life, stopping the aircraft from blowing away as the storm passed over and died away as the late summer's afternoon returned to tranquillity. Once it had, we flew back to Redhill—again, a lovely, dead calm, flight.

Well, I may have mentioned before that Biggin Hill at that time did not like microlight aircraft landing there, so even though the other aircraft (the Cessna from Redhill, an aircraft in a heavier weight category than the Shadow but nevertheless, only a two-seat single-engine aeroplane) had also made a precautionary landing, our flight was criticised. There was no problem with the Cessna, but Biggin Air Traffic Control created a Mandatory Occurrence Report against our little microlight and that report of course went off to the civil aviation authority; and I later received a letter summoning me to the CAA to explain why I had been flying in thundery weather.

Now, I will say at this point that I don't think that the two interviewers were nasty, but they evidently had to summon me to give me a rollocking. I was young, then, and they were older than I, and my father had always told me to respect my elders. So, I was eating humble pie until the two interviewers told me that I should not have landed at Biggin but instead carried on to Redhill Aerodrome. With respect to them, of course, that was wrong: and after hearing that, I gave them this scenario.

I said, "OK, you are in my shoes, the flying is dead calm, late afternoon, with clear skies all around for miles. Suddenly, flying gets unusually, extremely bumpy, you then see thunderstorms forming all around you."

I tell them that the choices before you are that you could try to head back to Redhill, dangerously flying through the circle of thunder clouds surrounding you and not knowing if, after miraculously making your way through those, there would be a dangerous thunderstorm over Redhill Aerodrome to greet you—or you could elect to land at Biggin Hill Aerodrome which is very close on your right-hand side. (This is exactly the sort of decision that the pilot-in-command of a passenger-carrying aeroplane might well be called upon to take at some point during a flying career). I asked the two gentlemen what they would do. They did not answer the question, but instead, still had the last word and told me not to do it again!

The Long Flight to Palma Majorca

Flying to Majorca with the CT Microlight: With now 36 years as a flight instructor, most of my logbook consists of flying lessons at Cloudbase Aviation, my flight school at Redhill Aerodrome. In fact, a trip to Goodwood or Headcorn for a student's cross-country training was about as far as I usually ventured. This was to change when I decided to fly our beloved CT2K GCDJF to Palma de Mallorca. Soon after the Christmas celebrations, my friend Anthony and I eagerly watched the weather forecasts looking for a weather window of a few days just before New Year's Day.

We knew from past years that once we got into the first weeks of January, we would probably be grounded and unable to do the trip at all. We particularly monitored the forecast winds over the Mediterranean as the winter Mistral wind can be strong; we saw forecasts for 40 to 60 knots if we got the timing wrong.

On 28th December, it looked like the weather we were after would appear and last hopefully for the duration of the trip. While I intended to leave on Monday 29th, Anthony suggested we cross the channel from Redhill Aerodrome to Le Touquet Sunday afternoon, suggesting that it would be better getting an early start in France on the Monday morning. This worked well with us leaving

Redhill Sunday afternoon around 2 pm after I did a flight plan, flying over Lydd at 4500 feet and tying down the aircraft in Le Touquet 75 minutes later.

Le Touquet is a lovely, lively seaside town, and we were spoilt for choice for both hotels and restaurants. We enjoyed an early evening stroll round the town, admiring the Christmas decorations and lights. The next morning, we were at the airfield early. We actually arrived an hour too early as everything was closed until 9 am. Happily, we were let in to a reception area by a kind office worker and thus avoid a long wait in subzero temperatures. We topped up the aircraft with fuel and set off shortly after 9 am en route to a friendly airfield just north of Toulouse called Albi Le Sequestre. This airfield is in a sheltered area away from the main effects of the Mistral. Being only 565 feet above sea level, it also offered the option of a relatively low route to the sea should the cloud base reduce to prevent passage over the higher ground to the east.

After taking off from Le Touquet, we headed south and then southwest along the coast. At one point, our heading was towards the Penly nuclear power station, and a Paris controller kindly warned us, but it was on our plan using Skydemon to turn south before the station heading towards Le Mans with the intention of landing at Le Mans if we needed a break or else continuing on towards Albi. Unfortunately, as we had decided to go on a weekday, we had to cross the ring of French military jet training airspace that magically disappears off the map at weekends. This was the hard bit of the route plan as it hits you twice, north and south. The weather was perfect; we flew mostly around 3000 ft apart from crossing the military zone, where we increased or decreased our height as required and kept a nice fast but not hammering speed for the CT2K of 100 knots and normal cruise 116 knots.

The CT is a very fast and comfortable aircraft with a huge cockpit and baggage bays for your belongings, so we found we could fly for 4 ½ hours effortlessly. It was interesting how Skydemon warned us of the danger areas en route, mainly power stations that day; we could see these clearly in the distance as we passed some of them with spectacular clouds of vapour rising from the cooling towers. I thought I might not last the duration of the flight without a toilet break, so I took an empty plastic milk bottle in case we needed it, but I am pleased to say we didn't use it.

We soon were passing near Toulouse airspace and approaching Albi, flying over the high ground into this lovely airfield bathed in sunshine. After landing and showing our insurance documents to Lesley, the air traffic controller, and then fuelling the aircraft ready for the short flight to Son Bonet Majorca, we used an online booking service to find a hotel in the town. I took the cowlings off for a look and to top up oil and water although none was required.

Lesley had allowed us to put G-CDJF in the hangar for the night, so the old girl was tucked up, and we set off to find our hotel. We knew Tuesday might be the only bad weather day, so it wasn't a surprise when Tuesday's weather was not flyable. Unfortunately, we had not realised that, when we planned our route, Albi in the valley had its own weather system and Tuesday, Wednesday, New Year's Eve, Thursday, the airfield was fogged in.

Every day Lesley told us, which didn't help morale, that while Albi was thick with fog, another airfield just 10 km down the road was bathed in sunshine and with a perfect forecast in Barcelona, Palma and France. We were not happy, to say the least. The weather was due to a high-pressure system (1041) stuck over south/central France. I had to cancel the New Year's Eve dinner party we planned to get to in Palma, and we nearly spent New Year in McDonald's but not quite.

The only consolation was we found a nice warm hotel the New Orleans in Albi, returning each evening to their surprise to book another room for the night after spending another wasted day at the airfield gazing into the fog. The temperature was below freezing most of the time, typically starting around -4 C in the early morning and maybe just breaking zero by mid-afternoon. Each day, we got the aircraft out of the hangar, prepped it for flight, warmed it up and then put it back in the hangar after a wasted day when the fog didn't clear. Even on New Year's Day, when the airfield wasn't manned, we were still kindly allowed to enter the facility with the coffee machine, full heating still running, and also not charging us full hangarage for the week. I can see now why everyone likes flying in France. They are so helpful and can't do enough for you. From time to time, we met people coming to the airfield to fly but, like us, being thwarted by the weather, just stayed for a coffee and a friendly chat. On Thursday evening, the weather forecast Meteoblue told us the temperature in Albi was going to warm up Friday from -4 degrees to + 9, so with clear skies that night, I was hopeful. The next morning, Friday, I looked out of the hotel window, and it was once again a pea souper.

I had now resigned to leaving the aircraft in France and getting a commercial airliner to Spain picking up GJF another time; after all, I couldn't stay in France forever, but nevertheless, Anthony and I walked to the airfield in the fog. Lesley didn't raise our hopes, telling us that her friend in the Met office said Albi would not go up to 9 degrees but instead stay at -4 degrees; nevertheless, once again, we got the aircraft out of the hangar put our stuff in the baggage bays and warmed it up ready.

But a stroke of luck, at 11:30, we could see the sun trying to break through the fog a small hole appeared, slowly growing and a larger square of blue sky appeared. We were out of there as soon as Lesley had filed our flight plan. Once again wearing our uninflated life jackets and with my Delorme Inreach emergency locator beacon around my neck, as soon as we got through the hole in the sky, it was like we were on another part of the planet into the tropics. We flew through the blue and headed southwest towards the Mediterranean, climbing to almost 6000 feet to clear the high ground.

Thereafter, we headed out to sea, talking to Barcelona ATC on our right, a long way distant. There was not much to see flying over the Mediterranean at 5000 feet following Skydemon's magenta line until I asked for permission to descend to avoid cloud near the island of Majorca. As we approached Alcudia, we turned west, heading towards Son Bonnet Aerodrome. We landed on Runway 23, having travelled for 2 ¾ hours Albi to Son Bonnet. Four days fogged in waiting to do just 2 ¾ hours bathed in sunshine to Palma. Total flight time I estimate 8 ½ hours start to finish.

Many thanks to the staff at Albi Le Sequestre for their hospitality and to the Hotel New Orleans for keeping us warm and fed. Albi does not seem to have many eating places so the New Orleans having its own restaurant was perfect for us. Negatives none, except the delay, because of the fog and the fact I only had two shirts; not many clothes thinking it would be a 2–3-day trip. Luckily, the radiators in the hotel were the old type, red hot for the cold weather, and I was able to wash and dry my clothes in the wash basin as I didn't have many spares.

Epilogue

Well, the dream goes on—and I will admit, it is occasionally a nightmare. This year, 2024, I will do my three-yearly flight instructor renewal test which is normally an all-day test.

You might think that having been examining for so long and tested for that so often, such tests might have been shown to be unnecessary—but you'd be wrong! It's very easy to develop bad habits, especially repeating the same tasks or processes routinely—so re-testing puts one on one's mettle, so to speak and refreshes one's knowledge which can only be a good thing.

During the (now) thirty-six plus years of training pilots, I have accumulated around five-thousand-five-hundred flying hours, each one flying in the sky with this light microlight aircraft, sometimes being bounced around like a butterfly in the wind.

I go back thirty-six years to when I first started teaching, when I met a gentleman who owned a 'flexwing' microlight aircraft factory. He said to me, "What the hell do you want to be an instructor for? They are all trying to kill you." How right he was! Since then, the rules, new regulations and what I see as sometimes nasty dealing are taking the fun out teaching for we instructors. I have always told people that if this were a business selling cabbages, you wouldn't do this tomorrow as there is no money in it. That said, flying as chief flying instructor and running my own flying school for thirty-six plus years has allowed me to do all these hours of exciting flying—those hours I would never have been able to have afforded to do otherwise.

To all of you wanting to fly—go for it. Flying is exciting to learn and to do recreationally; and then if you want to get a high salary and a lot less stress, don't settle for being an instructor—get your commercial licence!